KU-760-135

CONTENTS

[3]

Picking Losers . . . ?

The political economy of industrial policy

JOHN BURTON

Lecturer in Industrial Economics,
Department of Industrial Economics and Business Studies,
University of Birmingham

Published by
THE INSTITUTE OF ECONOMIC AFFAIRS
1983

First published in September 1983

by

The Institute of Economic Affairs
2 Lord North Street, Westminster,
London SW1P 3LB

© THE INSTITUTE OF ECONOMIC AFFAIRS 1983

All rights reserved

ISSN 0073-2818
ISBN 0-255 36165-3

Printed in England by
GORON PRO-PRINT CO LTD
6 Marlborough Road, Churchill Industrial Estate, Lancing, W. Sussex
Text set in 'Monotype' Baskerville

[5]

PREFACE

The *Hobart Papers* are intended to contribute a stream of authoritative, independent and lucid analyses to the understanding and application of economics to private and government activity. The characteristic theme has been the optimum use of scarce resources and the extent to which it can best be achieved in markets within an appropriate framework of law and institutions or, where markets cannot work, in other ways. Since in the real world the alternative to the market is the state, and both are imperfect, the choice between them effectively turns on a judgement of the comparative consequences of 'market failure' and 'government failure'.

In *Hobart Paper 99*, Mr John Burton analyses both the economics and politics of a form of government interference with the free working of the market which goes under the label of 'industrial policy'. Though that label is a post-1945 invention, the practice it denotes is a variant of an age-old route of state intervention in economic life. Whereas, prior to World War II, industrial policy was prosecuted largely through import tariffs and quotas, its main contemporary instrument is the injection of taxpayers' money into selected firms or industries. This shift in means has come about primarily as a result of international agreement among the advanced nations in the post-war period—notably under the aegis of the General Agreement on Tariffs and Trade and the Treaty of Rome—severely to curtail the application of tariffs and quotas to trade in industrial goods. Denied legal recourse to these devices by a constraining framework of treaty obligations, governments have sought to achieve the same ends by developing the lavish disbursement of overt and covert subsidies to industry to a fine art. Thus industrial policy has today become a major element of government economic policy.

Defining industrial policy as government intervention in the process of economic evolution, Mr Burton sets out to examine both why the 'subsidy morass' has come into being and what effects it has on the efficient functioning of the market economy. His point of departure is that, uninhibited, market

[7]

processes fulfil the task of economic 'natural selection' which weeds out unviable activities and releases economic resources for more productive employment elsewhere. Since change is ceaseless and pervasive, adaptation to it is a pre-condition of maintaining, let alone improving, living standards. Economic life, like biological life, must therefore be continually evolving.

Inseparable from the process of economic evolution is the occurrence of corporate loss-making and bankruptcy, the nature of which is widely misunderstood by the general public and largely neglected in academic writings on economics and business studies—partly because neo-classical economic theory is primarily concerned with optimisation or, more generally, with the *successful* performance of enterprises, and partly because businessmen are understandably less ready to provide researchers with material for case-studies about business failures than about business successes. It is therefore a valuable correction for Mr Burton to stress that winding-up does not mean the physical destruction of a company's assets, and nor does it necessarily entail the total dismemberment of a company. It is rather, he says, a process of re-organisation, re-valuation, and change of ownership.

Mr Burton divides contemporary industrial policy into two general classes—which he calls 'accelerative' and 'decelerative'—though he notes that the distinction is by no means always clear-cut. Accelerative industrial policy (popularly referred to as 'picking winners', an expression satirised in the title of this *Paper*) aims to stimulate the birth rate of new business ventures, while the decelerative kind seeks to reduce the death rate of senescent companies and industries. He judges both to be wasteful of economic resources and inimical to the health of the economy as a whole. Both distort market forces and hamper the necessary process of economic evolution. Whether financed by taxation, government borrowing or inflation, both have harmful first- and second-order effects on unsubsidised companies whose capacity to provide well-paid and secure jobs is thereby diminished. The principal obstacle to a general awareness of these consequences is that, whereas the jobs 'saved' or 'created' by industrial policy are visible, concentrated and immediate, the costs in terms of jobs correspondingly destroyed are hidden, diffused and long-drawn-out. Unfortunately, the jobs destroyed are the more productive ones—in otherwise viable companies which could

[8]

have passed the test of natural selection but cannot survive the ripple effects of *un*natural selection by government.

Mr Burton is particularly dismissive of the pretensions of politicians and bureaucrats to entrepreneurial acumen and managerial expertise. Given both the nature of their career training and the financial incentives to which they are subject, it flies in the face of elementary commonsense to believe they can 'pick winners' or fulfil the task of 'company doctor' more successfully than private entrepreneurs motivated by opportunities for profit and possessed of specialised knowledge of business methods and markets. It is a reliable rule-of-thumb that, if an enterprise—whether at birth or close to death—cannot attract private capital, governments step in only at great peril to the taxpayer. Unfortunately, governments enjoy the unique luxury of being able to compel *other* people to foot the bill for their bad investments. Gambling with other people's chips inevitably conduces to a degree of recklessness.

As economists are increasingly coming to appreciate, there is limited mileage in seeking to analyse and explain the contradictions and wasteful absurdities of industrial and like policies in terms of the teachings of standard welfare economic theory with its implicit assumption that politicians and bureaucrats strive merely to serve the general public interest. Might we not find a more rational explanation for their behaviour if we relax that assumption? In Section III of his *Paper*, Mr Burton does just that. Drawing on the insights of that new branch of economics known alternatively as the economics of politics or of public choice, he examines contemporary industrial policy as a product of the political market where government is viewed as a self-interested party and where the vote motive (as opposed to the profit motive) is the principal determinant of its behaviour.[1] Deftly, he shows how the interaction of vote-seeking governments and subsidy-seeking producer groups encourages selective government intervention in industry and diverts managerial and trade union resources from productive employment to lobbying for government favours; and how, under present fiscal arrangements, support-seeking governments have a political incentive to subsidise firms in marginal constituencies and conceal the cost by spreading it among

[1] For an introduction to the economic theory of politics, Gordon Tullock, *The Vote Motive*, Hobart Paperback 9, IEA, 1976, and James M. Buchanan *et al.*, *The Economics of Politics*, IEA Readings 18, IEA, 1978.

millions of taxpayers, consumers and savers in current and future generations.[1] And industrial policy has to be administered. So a large sitting army of bureaucrats is installed who then become an additional, organised and articulate, vested interest in the maintenance—indeed, expansion—of the subsidy machine.

Though calling for the abandonment of selective industrial policy, Mr Burton sees a clear role for government in facilitating economic evolution in the market. He sets out an ambitious agenda of imaginative proposals which go to the roots of much that is retarding the expansion of prosperity in this country: general measures to improve the economic, social and political environment for industry (such as constraining the size of the non-market sector) rather than selective interventions; the treatment of small businesses as a general experimental zone of the economy in which regulations and taxes are reduced to zero or the barest minimum; a balanced-budget rule (which, in the UK, would require the adoption of a written constitution); government vouchers to individuals and tax credits to companies to finance more re-training; giving away ownership rights in loss-making state enterprises to the general public; and an international disarmament agreement on non-tariff barriers to trade.

Although the constitution of the Institute obliges its Trustees, Directors and Advisers to be dissociated from the author's analysis and conclusions, this *Hobart Paper* is offered as an incisive and comprehensive critique of a major strand of state economic policy which, if the *general* public interest guided the actions of government, might itself have been subjected to a winding-up order long ago.

August 1983   MARTIN WASSELL

---

[1] John Burton has examined the effects of Britain's 'fiscal constitution' in Buchanan, Burton and Wagner, *The Consequences of Mr. Keynes*, Hobart Paper 78, IEA, 1978.

THE AUTHOR

JOHN BURTON was born in 1945, and educated at Worthing High School for Boys, the University College at Swansea, and the London School of Economics. Since 1979 he has been a Lecturer in Industrial Economics in the Department of Industrial Economics and Business Studies, University of Birmingham, having previously lectured at Southampton University (1969-70) and Kingston Polytechnic (1971-79). In the summer of 1981 he was a visiting research fellow at the Heritage Foundation, Washington DC, and in 1981-82 he was a Nuffield Foundation social science research fellow.

He is the author of *Wage Inflation* (1972); *The Job-Support Machine* (1979); *The Future of American Trade Unions* (1982); (with J. T. Addison) *Trade Unions and Society* (1983); and of articles in numerous journals. For the IEA he has previously written 'Are Trade Unions a Public Good/'Bad'?: The Economics of the Closed Shop', in *Trade Unions: Public Goods or Public 'Bads'?* (IEA Readings No. 17, 1978); (with J. M. Buchanan and R. E. Wagner) *The Consequences of Mr. Keynes* (Hobart Paper 78, 1978); 'Externalities, Property Rights, and Public Policy', in S. N. S. Cheung *et al.*, *The Myth of Social Cost* (Hobart Paper 82, 1978); 'Trade Unions' Role in the British Disease: An Interest in Inflation?', in *Is Monetarism Enough?* (IEA Readings No. 24, 1980); 'An Economic Commentary', in H. S. Ferns, *How Much Freedom for Universities?* (Occasional Paper 65, 1982); and articles in the *Journal of Economic Affairs*.

John Burton joins the Institute of Economic Affairs as a Research Fellow in October 1983.

ACKNOWLEDGEMENTS

The author would like to express his gratitude to Professors
S. C. Littlechild and A. L. Minkes, to two anonymous referees,
and to Martin Wassell, for their comments on an earlier draft
of this *Paper*. All errors remaining are the responsibility of
the author.

J.B.

I. ECONOMIC EVOLUTION IN THE MARKET ECONOMY

In the United Kingdom, and in many other Western European countries, industrial policy has become a major element of government economic policy. Moreover, in the United States there has been a growing debate over recent years as to whether America needs a more formal and extensive apparatus of industrial policy. The purposes of this *Hobart Paper* are to examine the nature, origins, and consequences of this type of economic policy.

Economic evolution sans industrial policy
The nature and rationale of industrial policy are examined in detail in Sections II and III. First, however, it is necessary to set the scene for that later discussion by examining the sources, aspects, and underpinnings of the process of economic evolution in a market economy where industrial policies pursued by government are completely absent. This is especially important since it is so little understood. Contemporary texts on micro-economics, for example, seldom draw explicit attention to the evolutionary process inherent in the market economy. Yet, despite this neglect, the evolutionary feature of the market economy is undeniably one of its most important facets. It provides a major source of the potential of the market economy for economic dynamism.

Three major facets of the market economy
The purpose of Section I is thus to draw out the nature of the process of economic evolution in the market economy. We proceed about this task by examining three facets of the latter: the price system as a co-ordinating device; the profit 'system'; and the process of economic evolution in the market.

(i) *The price system as a co-ordinating device: the invisible hand*
This facet of the market economy has been well-known, and endlessly analysed by economists, since the time of Adam Smith. Its essence is that the prices established by market forces act as a vast medium of communication between diverse

[13]

consumers and producers. Put another way, it is a means by which consumers are able to signal their preferences to producers, and producers are able to signal information about the cost of alternative choices to consumers. Thus, for example, a rise in the price of a commodity as a result of a shortage of it provides a signal and encouragement to consumers to use the item more sparingly *and*, simultaneously, stimulates producers to find ways of increasing the supply.

The price system provides not only the signals but also the incentives for consumers and producers to alter their behaviour so as to bring consumption and production decisions into a closer conjunction. Thus in a free market economy it acts, in Adam Smith's words, like an 'invisible hand'. It co-ordinates the plans and activities of a myriad of different economic agents, each of whom is acting on his or her own behalf, and obviates the need for anyone to be told what to consume or produce by some regulating authority. In so doing, the price system tackles the fundamental problem of a modern, highly complex economy: how, in a system with an intricate division of labour, the plans and activities of millions of separate individuals, each knowing little if anything of the detailed plans and activities of others, can be brought into some degree of correspondence and co-ordination.[1]

While there is general awareness that the price system has co-ordinative qualities, there is much less understanding—even amongst economists—of the nature of the co-ordination problem that the price system tackles or, more precisely, the conditions under which it operates. Many economists argue that the real-world price system does not function perfectly, in contrast to the textbook model of perfect competition. Government must therefore, they argue, step into the pricing system to make it work more perfectly.

It is quite true that the market economy may not generate perfect 'harmony', at all points in time, in the sense that no unrealised gains from trade exist.[2] Indeed, the conditions under which markets might result in such ideal outcomes are immensely stringent—and very implausible. They would, for

[1] For a brilliant analysis of this aspect of the market economy, the seminal paper by F. A. Hayek, 'The Use of Knowledge in Society', *American Economic Review*, Vol. XXXV, No. 4, September 1945, pp. 519-30.

[2] That is, in technical terms, the market may not always generate a Pareto-optimal allocation of resources.

example, require every market participant to be 'perfectly informed' about *all* prices in the (ever-changing) constellation of the price system (as they are assumed to be in the model of perfect competition, and in the Walrasian general equilibrium model).[1]

Real-world market processes cannot achieve perfectly harmonious outcomes because the assumption of perfect information is not valid in the real world. Indeed, it is precisely because we do *not* have perfect information that a market economy, which saves on the information costs of organising a complex economic system, is vital for the task of economic co-ordination. Whereas, in the textbook models of perfect competition and Walrasian general equilibrium, 'the' market is visualised as a method of allocating scarce means among diverse ends *when all relevant data are known by all market participants,* markets in real life are to be understood as a means of coping with our ignorance in a world of pervasive uncertainty.

(ii) *The profit 'system' of the market economy*

The second major facet of the market economy is also widely recognised. It has long been understood that a fundamental driving force for change and progress in a system of private enterprise is the search by entrepreneurs for opportunities for profit.

This is not to suggest that there is widespread understanding of the *nature* of profit (a topic to which we shall return later in this Section). Much public discussion of profit is bedevilled by fallacies about its origins and nature in a market economy—notably, different forms of the Marxian exploitation doctrine and the common confusion between the concepts of accounting profits and 'pure', or economic, profits.[2] There is, however, a general recognition among academic economists that the 'profit motive' is central to the workings of a private enterprise economy.

---

[1] In the Marshallian model of perfect competition all market participants are assumed to have perfect knowledge of all price offers, whereas in the general equilibrium model of market interaction erected by Walras, this information is assumed to be costlessly supplied to all participants by an all-knowing 'auctioneer' who co-ordinates the market.

[2] A useful textbook analysis of the many confusions surrounding the notion of profit is in J. F. Due and R. W. Clower, *Intermediate Economic Analysis,* R. D. Irwin, Homewood, Illinois, 1966, Ch. 17.

Under a system of private property rights, the owner of an enterprise is able to collect any residual between sales receipts and costs of production.[1] He thus has a strong and direct incentive to organise production and monitor the efficiency with which his enterprise uses resources with a view to maintaining, and indeed increasing, its profitability.[2] Two main methods are open to him to achieve such an outcome: the first is to be alert to consumer desires (and especially to currently unsatisfied desires); the second is to find new ways (including, for example, better systems of labour relations) of reducing the costs of production.[3] The profit motive thereby promotes responsiveness to consumer demands and the dynamic growth of efficiency.

The incentive to acquire profits, it should be emphasised, derives from the existence of marketable private property rights in the ownership (and thus ultimate control) of resources. If the rights were removed, so would the profit motive. It is for this reason that the idea of 'market socialism' is deeply flawed. Under such a régime, there would be no private ownership rights in enterprises; their assets would all be owned by the state. Yet their managers would be instructed to act *as if* they were profit-seeking entrepreneurs in a perfectly competitive market, setting prices equal to the marginal costs of production.[4] As in a free-market economy, demand and supply would be co-ordinated by price, but state boards would undertake the task of discovering and announcing market-clearing prices.[5] The flaw in such a system is that it cannot mimic the free market because it does not replicate the property rights arrangements from which the features of free-market processes derive. The managers of a state enterprise do not

---

[1] 'Costs' are to be understood here as the *opportunity* costs of production. Thus the costs of an enterprise, properly defined, include the interest foregone on capital employed and entrepreneurial quasi-wages.

[2] The idea of owners as 'monitors' is explored and developed in A. A. Alchian and H. Demsetz, 'Production, Information Costs and Economic Organisation', *American Economic Review*, December 1972, pp. 777-95.

[3] B. Ruml, 'The Profit Motive', in A. Klaasen (ed.), *The Invisible Hand: Essays in Classical Economics*, Henry Regnery, Chicago, 1965, pp. 158-65.

[4] The equating of market price with the marginal cost of production is the rule for profit-maximisation for a perfectly competitive enterprise.

[5] The idea of market socialism was advanced in particular by Oskar Lange: 'On the Economic Theory of Socialism', *Review of Economic Studies*, Vol. 4, No. 1, October 1936, pp. 53-71.

have the same incentive to be alert to consumer desires, or to introduce cost-cutting procedures and innovations, because they do not own, and thus cannot capture, any profits from their entrepreneurship. Instructing people to act as profit-maximisers is *not* the same thing as giving them the incentive to do so.

The neglected facet of the profit 'system': loss-making

There is another side of the coin to the profit system of the market economy which is perhaps less understood: the occurrence of losses, which often lead to business failure and bankruptcy. Time and again, public discussion overlooks that the market economy is not a machine which automatically distributes profits to the owners of enterprises; it is a system which throws up both profits *and* losses. Indeed, as will be shown later (pp. 18-21), the occurrence of losses is of fundamental importance to the evolutionary functioning of the market economy.

A lopsided view of the profit-and-loss system is not confined to the man in the street. The neglect of loss-making is also pervasive in the two academic disciplines which should be most concerned with the analysis of enterprise failure: economics and business studies. Thousands of books and learned articles have been written by economists about the growth and prosperity of the business enterprise. Only a few have addressed themselves to business failure. Even the most advanced texts on micro-economics seldom, if ever, mention the terms bankruptcy and liquidation. It is true that the economic analysis of profit does embrace the topic of loss-making in that a loss may be treated conceptually as a negative profit. Yet, while this treatment is formally adequate, it gives rise to habits of thought and discourse which tend to conceal the importance of business failure as a major component of the process of evolutionary change in the market economy. As this *Hobart Paper* argues, loss-making and the collapse of enterprise are central to that process. Their role should not be obscured by the analytical convenience of assuming that losses are merely positive profits 'with the sign reversed'.

Contemporary texts on business studies are only slightly better in this respect. Before the Second World War—influenced, no doubt, by the wave of American business failures during the 1930s—American texts on business finance used to devote considerable space to corporate bankruptcy and re-organisation. In the long period of general international prosperity which followed the war, however, enterprise failure was demoted in the literature. Despite the growing incidence of bankruptcies in America, Britain, and elsewhere since the late-1960s, the topic continues to be neglected in contemporary texts on business studies. Two reasons for this neglect deserve to be mentioned.

First, in the post-war period the teaching of business methods has made increasing use of quantitative economic techniques of decision-making such as portfolio analysis, linear programming, cost-of-capital theory, capital budgeting and valuation analysis. All these techniques are related to developments in quantitative economics. As already noted, contemporary economics is primarily concerned with optimisation or, more generally, with the successful performance of enterprises. Business catastrophes and collapses do not fit easily into such an optimising framework of analysis.[1]

A second reason for the continuing neglect of loss-making and enterprise failure in business studies is the lack of detailed case-studies. While histories of business successes and corporate growth abound, case-studies of liquidations and bankruptcies are rare.[2] Whereas businessmen are apparently willing to provide researchers with the details of successful ventures, they show—quite naturally—a marked reluctance to afford the same facilities when corporate mortality is under scrutiny. No-one likes to advertise failure.

The economic significance of loss-making and enterprise failure

There are a number of reasons why loss-making and enterprise failure ought not to be neglected.

First, they are a real and continuing feature of the operation of a market economy. Business firms are continuously changing, in much the same way as a biological species. 'Births' of new enterprises and 'deaths' of existing ones are occurring simul-

---

[1] Neo-classical market theory does treat the topic of enterprise exit from an industry, but says little about enterprise *mortality* and its systemic consequences.

[2] Two noteworthy books containing studies of enterprise failure are J. E. Ross and M. J. Kami, *Corporate Management in Crisis: Why the Mighty Fall,* Prentice-Hall, Englewood Cliffs, N.J., 1973, and A. F. L. Deeson, *Great Company Crashes,* W. Foulsham & Co., London, 1972.

taneously all the time. Commenting on the US statistics, Professor Altman has noted that 'the number of new businesses tends to exceed discontinuances each year by a small margin but . . . the aggregate flow is considerable'.[1]

The same pattern of flux in the population of enterprises is also true for the UK. In 1981, company 'deaths'—as measured by removals from the companies register (the best available measure)—totalled 29,739. Although insolvencies were very many in that year, so also were new company registrations: a total of 75,358 private and 58 public new companies were registered. In both 1981 and 1982, new registrations attained record levels.

The composition of the 'mortality rate' of business enterprises exhibits a clear tendency towards 'infant mortality': business failure is highly concentrated among the ranks of young firms. However, not even the largest of firms—unless they are nationalised or bailed-out by government subsidies—appear to be immune from the prospect of corporate 'death'. As Altman has recorded:

> 'During one week in June 1970, three large [American] companies petitioned the courts for protection under the Federal Bankruptcy Act. They included Four Seasons Nursing Centers, Dolly Maddison Industries and the grand-daddy failure of them all—Penn Central Transportation Company'.[2]

Since these corporate names have now passed into history, it is worth recalling the magnitude of the assets involved in that single week in the USA. In 1969 (and at 1969 US dollars), Four Seasons had assets of $37·7 million, Dolly Maddison $92·4 million, and Penn Central $4,700 million. The Penn Central collapse was the most spectacular corporate bankruptcy in history (to date). And in 1971, by only the narrowest of margins, the US Congress passed a bill guaranteeing loans to the Lockheed Corporation, which would otherwise have been driven into bankruptcy. Similar failures of corporate mammoths have occurred in Britain over the past decade, Rolls-Royce and British Leyland (in 1971 and 1974-75 respectively) being only the most spectacular examples. These two corporate giants continued in existence, without the form of re-organ-

---

[1] E. I. Altman, *Corporate Bankruptcy in America,* Heath Lexington Books, Lexington, Mass., 1971, p. 14.

[2] E. I. Altman, *ibid.,* p. xix.

isation which accompanies corporate bankruptcy, because of government intervention in the process of economic evolution. We shall return, in the major part of this *Hobart Paper*, to the advisability of such government action. At this point it is only necessary to emphasise once again that, in the absence of industrial policy, the disappearance or at least drastic re-organisation of loss-making private concerns—even of the largest companies—is a very real prospect in a market economy.

The second reason for not neglecting the failure of enterprises is that it has different characteristics from the process of business success and growth. Despite the simplification of much economic writing on profit and loss in the market economy, sustained loss-making which leads to the disappearance of firms cannot be viewed merely as profit-making 'with the sign reversed'. Bankruptcy is no more the opposite of profitability than death is the opposite of life. A very important asymmetry is entailed in the operation of the market economy, as with life and death. In the absence of government assistance, only enterprises which continue to make profits—or, at least, the prospect of eventual profits—survive. Those which incur sustained losses, and which have no prospect of a return to profitability, disappear. An underlying purpose of this *Hobart Paper* is to make clearer the *qualitative* significance of this aspect of the market economy.

Thirdly, and related to the foregoing point, the systemic consequences of enterprise failure are commonly misunderstood in much popular, political, and media discussion of the subject. Such discussion has a tendency to view the failure of a specific firm as damaging to the economy generally. This is especially so with the failure of a very large one; the imminent bankruptcy of Rolls-Royce in 1971, for example, was widely regarded in Britain as a national catastrophe. Clearly, any corporate bankruptcy is at least a minor calamity for the owners of the enterprise and for those who have contracts with it to supply labour or other resources. It is, however, insufficiently understood that the eradication of loss-making concerns also yields positive systemic consequences for the functioning of the economy as a whole.

So important is this issue that the study of business economics might arguably have been better served if economic theorists had focused their analysis of the market, not on the profit motive and profit-maximisation, but on how the market economy copes with and adjusts to the pervasive presence of business error and business failure.

The fourth reason why enterprise failure requires more serious examination is that it has become an increasingly important cause of government intervention over the post-war period. This matter will be examined in detail in Sections II and III.

(iii) *The process of economic evolution*

The discussion so far has led us by steps to the third major aspect of the market economy, which may be termed the process of economic evolution—a property of remarkably similar characteristics to the Darwinian concept of biological evolution. It is noteworthy that the idea of evolution was well understood by such 18th-century social theorists as David Hume and Adam Smith, and it is widely recognised that, in arriving at his theory of biological evolution, Charles Darwin was much influenced by such strands in socio-economic thought.[1] However, economists' understanding of the market economy as an evolutionary order faded out during the 20th century. It has now re-surfaced as the result of the work of Armen Alchian and Friedrich Hayek.[2]

The process of economic evolution in the market economy has two principal characteristics: business experimentation ('mutation') and economic 'natural selection'.

The market economy provides an opportunity for business experimentation which is absent from a centrally-directed economy. Entrepreneurs are not prohibited from creating new enterprises, attempting to sell new products, introducing new technology, trying out new employee relations practices and new marketing strategies, or whatever. All such activities might be conveniently summarised under the label of experiments or 'mutations' in business practice. Moreover, in contrast with Darwin's vision of biological evolution, 'mutation' in business enterprise is not confined to new firms; it can and

---

[1] This matter is described at greater length in F. A. Hayek, *Law, Legislation and Liberty*, Vol. I: *Rules and Order*, University of Chicago Press, Chicago, and Routledge & Kegan Paul, London, 1973, especially pp. 20-21.

[2] A. A. Alchian, 'Uncertainty, Evolution and Economic Theory', *Journal of Political Economy*, Vol. LVIII, 1950, pp. 211-21. Hayek's work on evolution in the economy and society is widely scattered throughout his writings; a useful introduction is in Ch. 2 of his *Law, Legislation and Liberty*, Vol. I, *op. cit.*

does occur in old, established businesses. For the behaviour of business enterprises is not determined genetically; it is the result of human choice and action, guided by decision-makers' perception of and alertness to opportunities.

The second principal characteristic of economic evolution is the process of economic 'natural selection'. As already noted, in a market economy where there are no government subsidies and 'soft loans' to failing enterprises, *only* those firms which are able to cover their costs with sales receipts survive in the long run. Conversely, firms which record persistent losses disappear. This is economic 'natural selection' at work.[1]

There are qualifications to be added to this bald statement about the process of economic 'natural selection'. A firm will go bankrupt only if it is unable to cover its contractual fixed costs, such as interest payments, out of its receipts (unless the owners are willing and able continually to cover the deficiency from their own pockets). The creditors then become the new owners of the assets. They may decide to re-organise the business more efficiently, put it (or parts of it) up for sale as a going concern, or sell off the assets individually to a variety of people. The course of action they choose will depend on their perceived return (or loss avoidance).

A different situation exists where a firm earns sufficient receipts to cover its contractual fixed and variable costs but not depreciation. That firm will not go bankrupt, but when its equipment wears out it will not have the funds to replace it. Unless a substantial improvement is anticipated in the returns to the enterprise, its owners are likely to wind it up voluntarily.

A third instance of discontinuance arises where the business produces enough revenue to cover contractual costs and depreciation charges but does not yield a sufficient rate of return on the money capital (and effort) invested to warrant carrying on. While such an enterprise might stay in business indefinitely, its owners are likely to wish to move their capital to where they can expect a higher return—in which case they will liquidate the enterprise voluntarily.

Through these various means, firms which are making losses—in the opportunity cost if not the financial sense—are 'selected out'. It must be emphasised, however, that economic 'natural selection' in the market economy does not necessarily

---

[1] The process of economic 'natural selection' was first analysed by Armen Alchian (1950), *op. cit.*

cause the immediate disappearance of a firm that is failing to cover its costs (including implicit costs, such as higher prospective returns elsewhere). Many businesses often go through short periods of technical insolvency, for example, but are able to stay afloat by borrowing to meet their cash-flow deficiency. For this to occur, they must be able to find lenders who have sufficient confidence in their long-run commercial viability and their capacity to repay the loan with interest.

Losses serve as an important warning light about an enterprise. While a loss may be due to purely temporary factors, soon to be reversed, it may also signify a deeper malaise in a firm, such as the wrong product line, management incompetence, excessive labour costs, or accounting laxity. At the very least, it is a signal to the owners, and those with whom they contract or borrow money from, to scrutinise the operations of the company more searchingly. If the difficulties are not temporary, the company must be re-organised—or the process of economic 'natural selection' will eventually come into play.

Enterprise experimentation and economic 'natural selection' together constitute the basic features of the process of economic evolution in the market economy. The former permits experimentation with new and untried products or techniques for producing products; economic 'natural selection' eventually weeds out unviable activities, thus deploying resources away from less efficient enterprises. This process is a main wellspring of progress in the market economy.

Although, in his original analysis, Professor Alchian seemed to imply that economic 'natural selection' would work over time to weed out all except profit-maximising businesses, it has been shown that this is not necessarily so.[1] Economic evolution does not ensure the 'survival of *only* the fittest', in the sense of perfectly profit-maximising firms. It leads only to the 'survival of the fitter' at any point in time. It cannot guarantee that all survivors are flawless specimens of business entrepreneurship and efficiency.

Finally, the idea of economic evolution in the market is not to be confused with the philosophy of 'Social Darwinism' which Herbert Spencer and others enunciated in the 19th

---

[1] S. G. Winter, Jr., 'Economic "Natural Selection" and the Theory of the Firm', *Yale Economic Essays*, Vol. 4, No. 1, Spring 1964, pp. 225-72.

century.[1] The Social Darwinists analysed evolution in society as a competitive struggle for existence among *individuals*; some even argued that anyone who could not earn a living was 'unfit' and should therefore be allowed to starve.[2] The process of market economic evolution analysed here differs from Social Darwinism. First, the analysis is concerned with the evolution of enterprises and their internal procedures, and not with the selection of individuals. Secondly, it is positive and not normative in orientation. It seeks to describe the evolutionary workings of the business sector in a market economy.

The inter-relation of the three facets

The three major facets of the market economy analysed above are inter-related.

Unlike the Walrasian auctioneer of general equilibrium theory, the price system of real-world markets does not flawlessly determine the equilibrium prices which will clear all markets simultaneously. Its nature is rather that of a device for coping with pervasive ignorance and uncertainty, and of economising on the costs of co-ordination under such conditions.

The occurrence of profits and losses flows from the nature of the price system or, more accurately, from the conditions under which it operates—conditions of perpetual change, and thus uncertainty and maladjustment. As Ludwig von Mises argued:

> 'If all people were to anticipate correctly the future state of the market, the entrepreneurs would neither earn any profits nor suffer any losses. They would have to buy the complementary factors of production at prices which would, already at the instant of purchase, fully reflect the future prices of the products. No room would be left for either profit or loss . . .
> '. . . Profit and loss are ever-present features only on account of the fact that ceaseless change in the economic data makes again and again new discrepancies, and consequently the need for new adjustments originate.'[3]

---

[1] H. Spencer, *The Man versus the State*, with an Introduction by A. J. Nock, Liberty *Classics* Edition, Liberty Fund, Inc., Indianapolis, 1981.

[2] Spencer himself specifically defended charity towards the poor as an evolutionary asset—provided 'it was not overdone'.

[3] L. von Mises, 'The Economic Nature of Profit and Loss', in his *Planning for Freedom*, Libertarian Press, South Holland, Illinois, 1974, pp. 108-109.

Business experimentation, which is one aspect of economic evolution in the market, is a principal source of change. The emergence of new products, new enterprises, new technologies, new methods of organisation or marketing, and so on, creates uncertainty about the future, for they are unpredictable. As in science, new ideas in business cannot be predicted accurately in advance. If they could be, they would not be new ideas.[1]

Economic evolution and the centrally planned economy

That analysis explains why, unless there is to be a considerable retardation of economic development—or, more probably, a severe decline in economic prosperity—the economy can never be computerised and the co-ordination problem solved by central planners. In principle, a sufficiently large computer system could solve the economic co-ordination problem in a *static economy*, provided it was fed *all* the necessary information (namely, the demand and supply schedules of every individual for every output and input). If no demand or supply schedule shifted, the 'solution'—the set of tasks, saving, consumption, and so on for every individual—could be determined. However, it would certainly not be possible in practice because of the gigantic problems of computation and of collecting, storing, and retrieving information.

Co-ordination by computer is not even *feasible in principle* in an economy in which new business ideas and products are allowed to emerge freely. Electronic computers can solve large-scale computational problems better than the human 'computer'. Like the latter, however, computers cannot predict in advance that which cannot be predicted by definition: new ideas. To cope with this problem, the computers of the planning agency would require to be told *in advance* what new products would be introduced over the planning period so that the Plan might allow for their impact. The question, however, is where these new business ideas might come from in a centrally-planned economy. Three sources suggest themselves.

Sources of business experimentation in the centrally directed economy

First, new ideas might be developed in pools of market activity outside the centrally planned economy, or in cordoned-off

---

[1] K. Popper, *The Poverty of Historicism,* Routledge and Kegan Paul, London, 1957, especially pp. v-vii.

zones within it. In these 'experimentation zones', new entre-preneurial ideas could be allowed to emerge and, if found successful or at least viable, could be incorporated into the Plan as new products. Incidentally, this solution renders world communism/central planning and economic progress in-compatible in principle.

Secondly, the central planners could themselves act as the source of new ideas about products and processes, and could programme them into the Plan. This procedure raises the important question whether it is better to have the task of entrepreneurship and innovation concentrated in the hands of a few individuals or divided up among many. It seems im-plausible that a few central planners would come up with the same variety of new ideas as the decentralised experimentation of a market economy produces. The poor rate of innovation of the politbureaus and central planners of Eastern 'bloc' régimes seems to bear this out.

Thirdly, the central planners might appoint an 'evaluation committee' to advise them on new enterprises, and invite individuals at large to present new ideas to the committee for its evaluation. However, in a centrally-planned economy—where profits (and losses) are by definition excluded—individ-uals would have no incentive to develop new business ideas and submit them to the committee. Even if this drawback was patched-over by rewarding individuals whose ideas were adopted with 'prizes', a problem of how the committee would evaluate enterprising ideas and decide which to accept and which to reject would remain.

Central planning lacks economic 'natural selection'

This lengthy detour about how a central planning régime might find sources of new enterprising ideas and accommodate them within the straitjacket of planned co-ordination, leads to the conclusion that there might possibly be ways of patching-on the introduction of new business developments to a central planning process without making central planning impossible. This, however, would only produce a further problem. While the central authority might be able to plan the introduction of new ventures, how would it decide *which* ones to introduce, and also when to discontinue them? In the absence of an objective market test, for example, there would be no way of knowing whether consumers really wanted a new product. The guesses of an evaluation committee would be no substitute for the information obtainable from exposing new ventures to real market forces, including the survival test of economic 'natural selection'. It is the absence of the 'natural selection' test which must ultimately be considered one of the most serious flaws in a fully-collectivised economy.[1] For such an economy has no way of diagnosing and eradicating enterprise failure. Compared with a market economy, its potential for economic evolution is thus significantly reduced.

The general theme restated

The three major facets of the market economy we have discussed—the price system, the occurrence of profits and losses, and the process of economic evolution—are interlocking, integral components of the market system. It is extremely difficult to envisage how one might be eliminated or stultified without dislocating the others and thus bringing the workability of the whole inter-related system into question.

This general analytical conclusion is of supreme importance for the discussion of industrial policy which follows. For industrial policy is, in effect, government intervention in the process of economic evolution. The fundamental question is whether such intervention is beneficial or whether it undermines the operation of the market system.

---

[1] G. W. Nutter originally called attention to this issue in 'Markets without Property: The Grand Illusion', in N. Beadles and L. Drewery, Jr., (eds.), *Money, the Market and the State*, University of Georgia Press, Athens, Ga., 1968.

II. INDUSTRIAL POLICY: GOVERNMENT INTERVENTION IN ECONOMIC EVOLUTION

The nature of industrial policy

Over the post-war period, and most notably in Western Europe, the governments of advanced mixed economies have interfered increasingly by various policy means in the process of economic evolution. Such policies go under a variety of names: adjustment assistance, industrial strategy, industrial regeneration, selective industrial assistance, structural and sectoral policies, and others. Here the term 'industrial policy' will be employed to include all such schemes.

Industrial policy may be defined as government intervention in the process of economic evolution.[1] The main instrument of contemporary industrial policy is the injection of taxpayer finance into selected firms or industries. This may occur in a variety of forms: outright industrial subsidies; labour subsidies to maintain jobs; state equity capital; or government loans, often with 'soft' (*i.e.*, subsidised) interest rates or repayment terms. Another widely-used, implicit means of subsidising selected firms is to give their tenders preferential treatment (over, for example, foreign competitors) in government purchasing decisions.

Although the term 'industrial policy' is a creation of the post-war period, the practice is not. On the contrary, it is one of the oldest forms of state intervention in Western countries. All that has changed is the form of industrial policy—the instruments government uses to interfere in the process of economic evolution. Prior to the Second World War, tariffs on imports were the main means of prosecuting industrial policy. However, under the aegis of the General Agreement on Tariffs and Trade (GATT), to which most Western countries are signatories, several rounds of multilateral trade negotiations during the post-war period have brought about significant and general reductions of tariff barriers to international trade

---

[1] A related definition of industrial policy is '. . . any government measure, or set of measures, to promote or prevent structural change': V. Curzon-Price, *Industrial Policies in the European Community*, Macmillan, London, 1981, p. 17.

[28]

in industrial goods. Moreover, another international treaty—the Treaty of Rome—which established the European Economic Community (EEC), has also restricted the ability of its member states to deploy industrial tariffs against each other. It is this constraining framework of international agreements that has caused Western governments to pursue contemporary industrial policies by non-tariff means, and specifically to have recourse to overt or covert subsidies to companies and industries. Some implications of this development for the international economy and polity are discussed in the next Section.

While industrial policy has changed in form, it also seems generally to have grown in importance during the post-war period and, specifically, throughout the 1970s. This has been particularly so for the West European steel and shipbuilding industries.

The two types of industrial policy

While the practice of contemporary industrial policy comprises a large variety of 'special measures', 'rescue packages', 'sector programmes' and such like, two general classes may be defined: (a) policies which are designed to accelerate the rate of (successful) business experimentation, and (b) policies which are aimed at thwarting, decelerating, or reversing the process of economic 'natural selection'. The first class of industrial policies is aimed at stimulating the birth rate of new business ventures, and the second at reducing the death rate of senescent enterprises and industries. In consequence, the first type may be labelled 'accelerative' industrial policy and the second 'decelerative' (they are sometimes also described as 'positive' and 'defensive' policies).

Accelerative industrial policy is intended to speed up the birth rate of successful ventures through a selective injection of taxpayers' money or the provision of special tax relief. Birth-rate policies are applied in practice in a variety of forms which might be summarised as the encouragement of the 'three Ns': the emergence and growth of *new enterprises* (otherwise known as small business policy); the introduction of *new technology* into existing firms; and the generation of *new industries* based upon advanced technology.

Decelerative industrial policy has the proximate aim of preventing the process of economic 'natural selection' from

[29]

working—that is, to prevent corporate liquidation or bankruptcy. Its instruments are applied typically to senescent industries and big 'lame duck' enterprises. Here, the injection of taxpayers' money is supposed to provide a 'breathing space' in which one or more of the 'three Rs' will happen: *rationalisation* —of size or product lines; *restructuring*—of industrial relations practices or subdivisions (perhaps through the divestment of parts of the company); or *rejuvenation*—through the introduction of new and better management or more up-to-date equipment. In the absence of government subsidy, failing enterprise *must* restructure, rationalise, rejuvenate—or be eliminated. Decelerative industrial policy is thus implicitly or explicitly aimed at slowing the pace of such changes to a rate which government or one of its agencies judges to be more desirable on political grounds.

The unclear reality of industrial policy

While a distinction can be drawn between accelerative and decelerative industrial policies at the level of abstract principle, any specific industrial policy may in practice have a mixture— indeed, a confused mixture—of rationales. One important study of British industrial policy has been led to conclude that:

'Industrial policy in the United Kingdom since 1960 can only be characterised as incoherent. The basic objectives have not been clear, trade-offs between competing objectives have not been calculated in advance, the relevance of intermediate to final objectives has been obscure, and the efficiency of the methods employed have been uncertain.'[1]

Specific examples of the confusion of objectives abound. Steel producers throughout Western Europe, for example, have been given large sums of taxpayer finance always ostensibly to rationalise and restructure the industry. Yet, in practice, this aid has often been used to avoid or reduce rationalisation;[2] 'adjustment assistance' has facilitated adjustment resistance. Moreover, the balance of objectives implicit in any industrial policy may often shift with a change in government—or even,

---

[1] G. Denton, 'Financial Assistance to British Industry', in W. M. Corden and G. Fels, *Public Assistance to Industry: Protection and Subsidies in Britain and Germany*, Macmillan, London, for the Trade Policy Research Centre, 1976, pp. 120-64.

[2] V. Curzon-Price, *op. cit.*, pp. 85-98, provides an admirable account of the incoherence of European industrial policy towards the steel industry.

indeed, during a single government's term of office in response to political pressures associated with the electoral calendar.

For these and related reasons, this *Hobart Paper* will not examine the precise mixture of objectives associated with specific industrial policies. The objective of this Section will be to analyse the general logic of industrial policy or, more specifically, the logic of the two classes of industrial policy distinguished above.

Welfare economics and industrial policy

An obvious starting point is welfare economics—the branch of their discipline to which many economists turn to determine the appropriate agenda for government micro-economic policy.[1]

The essence of welfare economics lies in identifying, in real-world markets, departures from (what is claimed to be) an ideal—technically, a Pareto-optimal[2]—allocation of resources. More accurately, the welfare economist is interested only in those Paretian optima which lie upon the social welfare frontier of society, that is, the set of resource allocations which would generate the highest level of welfare for society. The sufficient conditions for the existence of Pareto optimality are perfect competition in all lines of production and no (Pareto-relevant) externalities in production or consumption.[3] Where the behaviour of real-world markets diverges from the conditions defined by the concept of the Pareto optimum, 'market failure' is said to occur and it is then assumed that a *prima facie* case exists for government intervention to cure, remove, or somehow offset the effect of the 'failure'.

How might industrial policy be justified in terms of this

---

[1] Economists of classical liberal, Austrian and public choice persuasions are critical of the value of orthodox welfare economics as a basis for policy prescription. Introductions to these critiques are in C. K. Rowley and A. T. Peacock, *Welfare Economics: A Liberal Restatement*, Martin Robertson, London, 1975; S. C. Littlechild, 'What Should Government Do?', in S. C. Littlechild *et al.*, *The Taming of Government*, IEA Readings 21, IEA, London, 1979, pp. 1-15; and C. K. Rowley, 'Market "Failure" and Government "Failure" ', in J. M. Buchanan *et al.*, *The Economics of Politics*, IEA Readings 18, IEA, 1978, pp. 29-42.

[2] A Pareto-optimum is defined as a situation in which no re-allocation of resources could make any one individual better off without making someone else worse off.

[3] The concept of (Pareto-relevant) externalities refers to the existence of a divergence between (marginal) social and private costs, or between (marginal) social and private benefits, in any activity.

welfare analysis and 'market failure'? The general answer is: not very well. Welfare economics can be involved to justify subsidies to firms which are subject to decreasing long-run costs or which generate significant external benefits.[1] But it does not provide a justification for government bail-out operations in the absence of these conditions. Moreover, the distributional criteria consistent with welfare economics relate to the distribution of income between persons, not organisations. Thus welfare economics can be made to rationalise unemployment insurance and redundancy payments to individuals but not financial assistance to bankrupt enterprises.

The 'infant-industry' argument

In international trade theory, there is a long-established, if still highly controversial, argument for *tariff* protection of infant industries which are not competitive against established foreign producers but would become so if they could survive and expand to take advantage of economies of scale. As Dr Brian Hindley has, however, pointed out:

> 'The infant industry argument . . . provides no intellectual basis for subsidising new industries. Properly analysed, it proves to require some inappropriability to investment in the industry, and from an economic point of view, it will always be better to remove that inappropriability than to subsidise the industry.'[2]

The infant-industry proposition implicitly assumes that there are impediments which prevent entrepreneurs in the new industry from taking a sufficiently long view about the returns on investment which are to be expected, once economies of scale are achieved. Dr Hindley's argument is that the appropriate remedy is to remove the impediments—if such exist—rather than indulge new industries by domestic protection. Sheltered industrial infants often do not 'grow up'.

The case for accelerative industrial policy

No clear argument for the accelerative type of industrial policy can be found in the literature of economics. It is therefore

---

[1] The standard argument for subsidising such activities is presented in any welfare economics textbook; an example is P. Bohm, *Social Efficiency: A Concise Introduction to Welfare Economics*, Macmillan, London, 1973, Ch. 2.

[2] B. Hindley, 'The Mixed Economy in an International Context', in E. Roll (ed.), *The Mixed Economy*, Macmillan, London, 1982, p. 198.

necessary to try to construct a logic for it out of government statements which accompany the introduction of assistance schemes.[1]

The implicit logic of accelerative industrial policy appears to derive from the (correct) recognition that new business experiments are the seed-bed for future economic development. For development to occur, new enterprises must come into being and be tested in the market-place; new technology must be tried out and, if successful, permeate the economy; new industries must spring up to replace those in decline. The use of government subsidies to promote enterprise birth and business mutation is based on the premise that government can act as the institutional equivalent of an incubator—that certain 'seedling' enterprises or industries be selected out and given especially favourable environmental conditions.

The odds against 'picking winners'

The principal drawback to such a strategy is that not all new businesses become successful commercial enterprises. On the contrary, the record of business failures is dominated by 'infant mortality'. How to 'pick the winners' out of the crop of new businesses poses, therefore, a major problem. It is easy to 'pick' winners once they have demonstrated their ability to reach the winning post, but extremely difficult to do so before the race has started.

Many new businesses which initially look promising prove to be flops. Some which look unlikely to take off successfully eventually do make it. There is no way of determining these matters in advance of the realisation of success or failure.

The selection of new businesses or new technologies to back with taxpayers' money is essentially a matter of judgement, hunch and gambling. Government cannot draw upon 'scientific' advice for the simple reason that no such 'scientific' expertise exists. There may be people—entrepreneurs and business policy experts—who have good hunches about new business; but, again, this can only be demonstrated after the event.

[1] Government policy towards new companies is examined at more length in M. Binks and J. Coyne, *The Birth of Enterprise*, Hobart Paper 98, IEA, 1983. The specific use of industrial policy to promote the development of advanced-technology enterprises is critically, and most lucidly, discussed in J. Jewkes, *Government and High Technology*, Third Wincott Memorial Lecture, Occasional Paper 37, IEA, 1972.

Any subsidy policy to promote enterprise birth will inevitably subsidise many eventual business failures.[1] Government should certainly seek to dismantle *barriers* to new entrepreneurship. And since a considerable proportion of such barriers stem from the activities of government—taxation, regulations, and local planning requirements—government can there do something unambiguously beneficial to encourage business experimentation.

The case for decelerative industrial policy: government as company doctor?

Government intervention to prevent economic 'natural selection' might be described as the 'government-as-company-doctor' notion. Company doctors are a type of consultant in the business world who specialise in restoring ailing companies to health. They are not hired by vigorous and highly successful corporations. As in the medical world, they are called in to deal with the sick.

Underlying the subsidised conservation of loss-making firms is the apparent assumption that the government, or one of its agencies (such as a state holding company), can act like a company doctor, restructuring the operations or management of the enterprise to restore it to profitability. Meanwhile, subsidies are necessary to stave off bankruptcy.

This view of supportive intervention has been advanced, for example, by Francis Cripps, a Cambridge economist who at one time advised the Department of Industry:

'In many industries the long-run prospects of individual firms tend to improve or worsen with cumulative effects. Initial success provides the opportunities for exploiting economies of scale and specialisation, together with profit and easy access to external finance needed to fund continual expansion. In this situation continued productivity improvements will follow as a result of growth from an initially advantageous position. On the other

---

[1] The experience to date of the small firms loan scheme in Britain is illustrative. Under the scheme, which became operational in 1981, commercial banks are encouraged to lend to small firms by a government guarantee to cover 80 per cent of any losses incurred. The senior general manager of Barclays Bank, Mr John Quinton, has disclosed that one in five of the companies lent money by his bank under the scheme failed. Barclays is the second largest lender in the scheme. ('One in Five Failure for Small Firms Scheme', *The Times,* 12 August 1982.)

[34]

hand, initial failure results in continued slow growth, lack of finance, inability to re-organise and low productivity growth.

'This analysis provides a justification for any form of subsidy which is sufficient to set a firm or industry on the path of sustained expansion. It is an argument for selective, temporary subsidies to rescue industrial invalids and restore them to health—after which they should be able to survive and prosper without further aid.'[1]

The attraction of such an argument to government appears especially strong in the case of *large* ailing enterprises. The reason usually offered is that government has 'no option' but to bail out insolvent companies when they are massive. Their collapse would cause large-scale redundancies, not only among their own workers but also in enterprises supplying them and in yet others supplying the latter (and so on). The 'ripple effect' of a major corporate crash, it is argued, could trigger bankruptcies and unemployment of tragic proportions. At the time of BL's impending failure in 1975, for example, it was claimed that its collapse would 'put one million jobs at risk' and lead to the 'desertification' of the industrial West Midlands. (Subsequently, the 'Ryder plan' was announced to inject £1 billion of taxpayers' money into the ailing car giant.)

Thus the argument for government as 'company doctor' assumes particular significance in the case of the very large enterprise. Here, the potential downward cumulative effects— inside and outside the company—are assumed by some to be so extensive as to make any other course of action 'politically impossible'.

Flaws in the argument for decelerative industrial policy

The logic of Cripps's 'cumulative effects' argument for industrial policy to avert enterprise morality is severely flawed on a variety of counts. First, it is quite unreal to divide business firms into two types, namely, 'expanders' and 'contracters'. Cripps's analysis presumes that enterprises are locked into either a 'virtuous circle' of ever-strengthening performance and exponential growth or a 'vicious circle' of plummeting decline ending in corporate failure. This is simply erroneous. Many firms wobble between periods of profit and periods of

[1] F. Cripps, 'The Economics of Labour Subsidies', in A. Whiting (ed.), *The Economics of Industrial Subsidies*, HMSO, London, 1976, pp. 105-108.

[35]

loss. Some achieve spectacular growth and then collapse: the story of the John Bloom washing-machine empire in the 1960s is one example of this phenomenon, and the more recent collapse of Dickie Dirt's cut-price clothing business in 1982 is another. Other enterprises sometimes go through long periods of decline and then achieve a sharp turn-around—frequently as a result of new management or ownership. The general point is that the processes of expansion and contraction of companies are very often *not* cumulative and *not* in one direction only.

Secondly, the 'cumulative effects' argument provides no justification for government subsidies as such. As Keith Hartley has noted:

> '. . . if industrial invalids restored to health are supposed to survive and prosper without further aid, why are subsidies required: why not loans?'[1]

Indeed, to carry that argument further, the case for merely government *loans* to industrial invalids is not clear. Finance is available in the market, even to companies with cash-flow problems, *provided* lenders can be assured that there are reasonable prospects of a return to profitability. If the company is diagnosed as being only in temporary difficulties, it should be able to borrow on the market. Conversely, a reluctance on the part of bankers to lend to a company in cash-flow difficulties is a sign that they do not assess the longer-term prospects of the company as sufficiently bright.

Can government make accurate forecasts of corporate performance?

When private lenders are unwilling to advance finance to an ailing company, the provision of loans by government must rest on the implicit premise that it can make better forecasts of corporate performance than operators in financial markets.[2] Here the experience of the National Enterprise Board (NEB), established in 1975 with over £1 billion of taxpayers' money, is instructive.[3] Among other things, the NEB was supposed to

[1] K. Hartley, 'The Economics of Labour Subsidies: Comment', in A. Whiting (ed.), *ibid.*, pp. 109-112.

[2] J. Wiseman, 'Is There a Logic of Industrial Subsidisation?', in K. Hauser (ed.), *Subsidies, Tax Relief and Prices*, Editions Cujas, Paris, 1981.

[3] The NEB was merged in 1981 with the National Research Development Corporation to form the British Technology Group.

act as a company doctor, turning round ailing companies which it assessed to have good long-term prospects. Its track-record at this task was dismal. In the year to December 1978, for example, the NEB reported a net loss (after accounting for extraordinary items) of £40·3 million. As Grylls and Redwood noted with studied understatement, 'this was not a handsome return on £1·4 billion'.[1] The performance of the Istituto per la Ricostruzione Industriale (IRI), the Italian state holding company, has been even more woeful. By the end of 1978, its accumulated debts totalled $21,000 million.[2]

In the light of such experiences, there must be very serious doubt that government, or its appointed agency, can act as an efficient company doctor. These instances highlight the danger that, instead of promoting economic evolution, industrial policy to avert enterprise mortality may undermine the process of economic 'natural selection' and thus damage general economic performance.

The fundamental problem to which the above discussion points is precisely the same as with accelerative industrial policy. Government cannot pick winners because there is no means available of predicting which companies will be winners. Likewise, government cannot fulfil the function of company doctor which can transform 'losers' into 'winners' because there is no science of 'company doctoring' on which it can draw for guidance. In medical science, there are, at least some-times, known cures for diseases or afflictions. Under such circumstances, it is possible successfully to treat physical illness by applying standard procedures laid down in the medical texts (although, of course, medicine is not an exact science either). The literature on business economics, however, will be searched in vain for panaceas certain to transform loss-makers into profitable enterprises. To put the argument another way, company doctoring is a form of entrepreneurship, resting ultimately upon an individual's alertness to, and insight into, the opportunities for successful re-organisation.

Business economics, or economic analysis more generally, is unable to provide either government or private entrepreneurs

---

[1] M. Grylls and J. Redwood, *National Enterprise Board: A Case for Euthanasia*, Centre for Policy Studies, London, 1980, p. 55.

[2] *Quarterly Economic Review*, Economist Intelligence Unit, London, No. 2, 1979, p. 14.

with detailed guidance on these matters. As Professor Assar Lindbeck has pointed out:

> '. . . the extreme micro-character and specificity of knowledge and competence required for successful entrepreneurship are so great that general deductions on the basis of economic analysis, including trade theory, are of rather limited interest for individual firms . . . when studying the "fine" structure of production, the comparative advantages are too complex to be explained or predicted either by central planners or by academic economists with the help of available methods of analysis.'[1]

The general conclusion is that neither received economic theory nor everyday experience offers any ground for the belief that government can, in formulating corporate forecasts, avail itself of 'scientific' expertise superior to that possessed by individuals with specialist and entrepreneurial abilities as company doctors. The claim that government is a better forecaster rests ultimately upon the supposition that it is, or can be, a superior entrepreneur to those operating in the market.

The concept of government as superior entrepreneur

It cannot be proved by logic that politicians and bureaucrats are better or worse as company doctors than those operating in the market itself. Two factors, however, strongly suggest that they are likely to be inferior.

First, the opportunities and incentives facing the two differ. The market entrepreneur who successfully re-organises a company can generate a profit for himself varying according to the volume of its shares he holds. In contrast, politicians and bureaucrats advance taxpayers' money and cannot, therefore, reap any profit from successful re-organisation (nor do they bear any personal financial loss from failure). Economists generally would agree that entrepreneurial alertness is stimulated by the opportunity of making profits; indeed, the very nature of entrepreneurship might be defined as the faculty of perceiving an opportunity for profit-making.[2] Thus, the private entrepreneur has a direct financial stake in the suc-

---

[1] A. Lindbeck, 'Industrial Policy as an Issue in the Economic Environment', *The World Economy*, Vol. 4, No. 4, December 1980, p. 394.

[2] For a penetrating discussion of the nature of entrepreneurship, I. M. Kirzner, *Competition and Entrepreneurship*, University of Chicago Press, Chicago, 1973.

cessful re-organisation of an ailing company whereas the politician or bureaucrat does not.

The second factor is the differential knowledge possessed by politicians and bureaucrats on the one hand, and market entrepreneurs on the other. Political careers are shaped in the political market, and politicians have a direct incentive to acquire a highly detailed knowledge of its complex workings. The bureaucratic career is moulded within bureaucratic hierarchies, which have their own complex conventions and procedures and which often differ considerably from bureau to bureau.[1] Knowledge of these conventions and procedures partly determines an individual's progress through the bureaucratic hierarchy. The bureaucrat has an incentive to invest in the acquisition of this highly specific knowledge in a way that, say, a motor mechanic or a commodities broker does not.

Likewise, the income (and status) of a private entrepreneur is determined by his performance in the market arena, and he has every incentive to acquire a highly detailed knowledge of the business activities in which he is involved—what Lindbeck calls the 'fine structure of production' (which includes, for example, the potentialities of employees and partners; the informal industrial relations system in operation in the business; and the possibilities of technical development and cost-cutting).

Time spent in acquiring detailed, highly specific knowledge has an opportunity cost in terms, among other things, of acquiring less of other forms of knowledge. We would thus expect entrepreneurs to have much larger stocks of highly specific knowledge about the 'fine structure of production' and of market opportunities than do politicians and bureaucrats.

Thus, on the counts of both incentives and specific knowledge —which are intimately connected matters—we would expect politicians and bureaucrats to be inferior to market entrepreneurs in the task of market entrepreneurship, including corporate re-organisation. This may seem like a statement of the obvious—of course motor mechanics do not make good brain surgeons (and *vice versa*). But it should be remembered that the argument for government intervention in the process of economic evolution is based on the implicit assumption that

[1] The administrative procedures in different university bureaucracies, for example, often differ considerably.

government is a superior entrepreneur to those available in the market. The motor mechanic has enough sense not to *seek* to perform brain surgery!

Buying-in entrepreneurial expertise

Cannot government overcome the problem diagnosed by hiring highly experienced and successful market entrepreneurs to sort out troubled industries and enterprises on its behalf? This question—which contains a more sophisticated argument for government intervention in the process of economic evolution than the assertion that government itself is superior at the entrepreneurial task—can only be answered by recalling the fundamental aspects of entrepreneurship: an alertness to opportunities, the incentive and opportunity to acquire entrepreneurial profit, and a highly detailed knowledge of the market in which the opportunities perceived exist. Successful entrepreneurship requires not simply 'alertness'. Without the possibility of personal profit, there would be less incentive to be entrepreneurially alert; and without detailed knowledge, opportunities would be less likely to be perceived in the first place.

The fundamental drawback of the 'buying-in' solution to overcome the lack of entrepreneurial talent in political and bureaucratic ranks is that it subverts the incentive precondition for successful entrepreneurship. Furthermore, it does not necessarily satisfy the precondition of detailed knowledge.

'Buying-in' entrepreneurial talent transmogrifies the successful businessman into a salaried bureaucrat. As an advisory official in a government agency or state holding company, he is no longer an entrepreneur. Like any other bureaucrat, he is unable to reap personal pecuniary profit from a successful corporate re-organisation. His salary remains the same whether or not he turns a company round, and his incentive to act entrepreneurially is reduced to that extent.

One way of meeting this objection might be labelled the 'MacGregor approach'—so-called after the terms of the appointment of the current chairman of the National Coal Board, Mr Ian MacGregor, to the chair of the British Steel Corporation (BSC), in 1980. When he was appointed, it was announced that his remuneration would be linked to the performance of BSC. Whilst this arrangement caused a considerable political furore at the time, it points some way towards satisfying the incentive pre-condition. But it also raises an important question—at least as far as government rescue operations in the private sector are concerned. If incentives must be maintained to ensure successful entrepreneurship—and this is the premise of the 'MacGregor approach'— why is government intervention necessary at all? The incentive for an entrepreneur to re-organise a company successfully will be maximised if he has ownership rights in it. In this way, he will capture the profit of his success. The ownership rights might be acquired (at a low price compared with what the entrepreneur perceives their likely worth to be after re-organisation) prior to liquidation; or the entrepreneur might purchase the assets of the enterprise after it has been liquidated. The 'MacGregor approach' therefore raises the question why corporate re-organisation is not allowed to proceed under straightforward market conditions.

Loss-making *state* enterprises (such as the BSC) present a different problem. Here, an entrepreneur-cum-company doctor who believes the enterprise could be successfully re-organised cannot purchase the ownership rights on the stock market because all the shares are owned by the state and there is no market in them. Moreover, many state enterprises (at least in Britain) are under a statutory duty to maintain the supply of their services; thus they cannot be discontinued or liquidated.

But to state these matters relating to public enterprises is simply to raise the question of their continued existence. If government wishes to see a successful re-organisation of loss-making state enterprises, why does it not remove their statutory duty to supply and then sell off the ownership rights in them? In other words, instead of *hiring* Mr MacGregor to re-organise BSC, an alternative solution would have been to let him (or others) acquire the ownership rights in it and proceed with re-organisation as owner(s), thereby maximising his (their) incentive to turn the Corporation round successfully.

Can loss-makers be sold?

One apparent barrier to this course of action is the belief in some political quarters that it is impossible to sell the ownership rights in loss-making state enterprises because no-one would want (or perhaps be foolish enough) to buy them. When

Secretary of State for Industry, Sir Keith Joseph told the 1980 gathering of the Mont Pèlèrin Society that this was the reason for not seeking to privatise BSC.

This notion is incorrect. It is not true that all loss-making enterprises have a zero or negative value, and thus cannot be sold at a positive price. The price an entrepreneur is willing to pay for a loss-making enterprise is determined not by its current performance but by his estimate of what the assets would be worth after re-organisation. One possibility would be for him to sell off the physical assets of the enterprise to others. Alternatively, having acquired the ownership rights, he may wish to keep the enterprise (or parts of it) as a going concern with a view to undertaking internal re-organisation—of the product line, marketing strategy, management team, manning arrangements, and so on. Whatever his precise strategy, the argument is that loss-making enterprises can be sold at a positive price provided someone perceives the potential of profit after re-organisation or asset disposal.

Horses for courses

Entrepreneurs are successful in one or a few lines of business; they cannot be so in all. This is because successful entrepreneurship is based upon highly specific and detailed knowledge of the 'fine structure of production' within a particular market context—knowledge which it takes years of involvement to acquire and much of which is so specific that it is not transferable to other types of business. The 'fine structure of production' in the restaurant business, for example, is quite different from that in ball-bearings, or micro-electronics.

This presents a further objection to the idea that government should 'buy-in' entrepreneurial talent to conduct industrial policy for it. If government hires businessmen who have had a successful career in, say, the chemical industry or in supermarket retailing, they may well—indeed, are most likely to— lack specific knowledge of the wide range of enterprises they are called upon to re-organise and bring back to profitability— electronics, computing, aero-engineering, bio-engineering, and so forth. The assessment of an enterprise's potential is not simply a matter of acquaintance with its accounts and a few other quantitative indicators; the possibilities of re-organisation can best be comprehended by those who best know the particular business, its market, and technological context.

[42]

The entrepreneurs who are likely to have the keenest appreciation of the possibilities of successfully re-organising a failing company are likely to be already active in the same (or a related) industry. This consideration reinforces the argument for allowing them to make the decision with their own money rather than appointing them as government agents and thrusting them in armed with taxpayers' funds.

On the maintenance of 'unique' teams or capital structures

Decelerative industrial policy, as opposed to re-organisation through bankruptcy, is sometimes advocated on the ground that a unique combination of specialist skills and/or types of capital equipment is embodied in a particular company. At the time of the Rolls-Royce crash in 1971, for example, it was claimed in some quarters that the company—being the only aero-engine manufacturer in Britain—had uniquely qualified and highly-trained staff, and that to let it collapse would mean the loss of this talent.

This argument implicitly assumes that a company which goes into bankruptcy is always broken up, its assets sold off to a diversity of other interests, and its employees scattered to a variety of other employments. The assumption is, however, wrong. The value to others of a bankrupt company is often greater if its assets and workforce (or part thereof) are maintained intact. The liquidator or receiver is therefore able to sell the whole enterprise, or major parts of it, as a going concern. Thus, in the re-organisation following the collapse of Laker Enterprises in February 1982, for example, the official receiver was able to sell off the package-holiday end of the business as an operating unit.

There is widespread misunderstanding about the nature of corporate liquidation and bankruptcy. Winding-up a business does not mean the physical destruction of the company's assets. All that happens is a change in the ownership of the assets and their simultaneous *re-valuation* (downwards). Nor does winding-up necessarily entail the total dismemberment of the company. If the new owners estimate that its assets are more valuable by being kept together, they have every incentive to do just that. Likewise, if there are good reasons for retaining the specialist skills of the current workforce, then they will seek to do so.

[43]

Corporate winding-up is a process of re-organisation, re-valuation, and change of ownership. It is not a process of destruction.

The counter-productive effect of subsidised 'breathing spaces'

The idea of decelerative industrial policy is to create a 'breathing space' in which re-organisation and rejuvenation of an enterprise can take place. The provision of subsidies in order to create the breathing space, however, reduces the incentive to re-organise and thus runs counter to the very purpose of the policy.

An ailing company which is facing potential bankruptcy knows that it *must* re-organise its activities and improve its performance. It is the very urgency of the situation which provides the stimulus to contemplate and implement drastic recovery measures. A company that is bailed out by government subsidies has, by comparison, much less incentive to re-organise: the threat of imminent disaster for its owners and controllers is suspended or at least diminished. The subsidised enterprise is consequently less likely to contemplate and undertake the requisite corrective measures. Moreover, subsidies encourage union negotiators to resist slower wage growth (or wage reductions) and de-manning, whilst taking the pressure off management to push for them as a component of the re-organisation and recovery strategy.

The hidden costs of delayed re-organisation

Expensive bail-outs which permit large loss-making enterprises to delay adjustment impose hidden costs on the rest of the economy. Ultimately, they handicap the performance of more efficient firms which survive without subsidies.[1]

The nature and distribution of this burden on the rest of the private sector will depend on a variety of factors, including how government chooses to finance the subsidies (as between taxing, borrowing from the public, and borrowing from the commercial banking system). If government raises income tax, for example, the *direct* impact will fall on the pockets of taxpayers. But there will also be a second-order effect on enter-

---

[1] A more extended discussion of these matters is in Victoria Curzon-Price, 'Alternatives to Delayed Structural Adjustment in "Workshop Europe" ', *The World Economy*, Vol. 3, No. 2, September 1980, pp. 205-15.

prises as tax-paying consumers reduce their expenditure on a variety of goods and services. Alternatively, financing the subsidies by an increase in the public sector borrowing requirement will tend to raise interest rates, and so complicate life directly for firms with outstanding borrowings. Moreover, the rise in interest rates will pull up mortgage rates, thus reducing the discretionary incomes of home-owners who will, in turn, have to reduce their demand for other goods and services.

Little specifically can be said about the burden imposed on the rest of the economy by decelerative industrial policy, except that it is real and must, in one way or another, reduce the prospects of more profitable enterprises in the economic system. Indeed, it may precipitate difficulties for many of them, even leading sometimes to failure. These are the hidden side-effects of decelerative industrial policy which do not make the newspaper headlines.

The fallacy of the ripple effect

While advocates of bail-outs may acknowledge that the propping up of large loss-making enterprises imposes burdens on the rest of the economy, they will argue that the ripple effect of letting them go to the wall (in terms of bankruptcies and redundancies among suppliers) also has a cost which must be set against the financial cost of propping up. The argument is, however, fallacious. It ignores the fact that imposing a burden on other sectors of the economy will also cause ripple effects to emanate from *them*. The logic of this proposition is implicit in the immediately foregoing analysis.

The economic agents (taxpayers, enterprises, consumers) on whom the burden of the state propping-up operation falls will have to reduce their expenditures to match the enforced reduction in their disposable incomes. This reduction in their expenditures will lower the sales of a large variety of firms which will in turn have to trim back on their operations. Employees may be laid off, in which case their incomes—and therefore expenditures—will fall. And suppliers will be hurt—some badly enough to force them to trim back on *their* operations . . . and so on in a long chain throughout the economy. Decelerative industrial policy financed by taxes imposed on others has the immediate effect of bailing out loss-making enterprises by imposing the burden of adjustment on others. Its secondary effect is to substitute one chain of multiple redundancies and bankruptcies for another.

It is thus quite wrong to maintain that the bailing-out by subsidy of a large loss-making enterprise is essential to avert a damaging ripple effect. It does no such thing. It simply, and artificially, causes the ripples to occur in other sectors of the economy which are not the source of the fundamental problem.

In general, we cannot say which of the two ripple effects—the averted or the imposed one—will be the larger in terms of redundancies and secondary bankruptcies. Many factors will determine it.[1] What *can* be stated with certainty is that de-celerative industrial policy financed by taxation triggers a ripple effect. Moreover, as we shall see in Section III, the incentive structure facing political and bureaucratic decision-makers is such that the ripple effect produced by decelerative industrial policy is likely to be diffused and thus 'hidden'.

If bail-outs are financed by money creation rather than by taxation, both Keynesians and monetarists tend to agree that there is at least a temporary net stimulative effect on the economy in conditions of less-than-full employment—although monetarists would argue that this fillip will fizzle out once the economy has adjusted fully to the monetary injection. The fillip to the economy would, however, have been bought at the long-run cost of inducing a mal-investment of resources in loss-making activities. While Keynesians argue that government should seek to stimulate the economy by means of monetary injection at times of recession, they do not argue that it should be done in such a way as to damage long-run growth prospects. The declared purpose of stabilisation policy is to stabilise the economy—not to sow the seeds of its stagnation.

Conclusion

The logic of accelerative industrial policy founders on the fundamental problem that, in the business arena, there is no magic formula upon which government can draw in order to

---

[1] This conclusion is not contradicted by the balanced-budget multiplier theorem of Keynesian economics. The theorem states that in the case of increased government subsidies financed by an equal tax increase, the economy will be stimulated only if the marginal propensity to spend of the recipients of the subsidy is larger than those who pay the increased taxes. There is no reason to assume that this would be so in the typical government bail-out.

[46]

'pick winners'. The case for decelerative industrial policy, based on the idea of government as company doctor, is similarly flawed; and in numerous ways.

The case against industrial policy is simple. The process of economic evolution serves an invaluable purpose; government industrial intervention thwarts it. Economic evolution in the market, which incorporates the process of economic 'natural selection', poses a survival test for all enterprises. The function of the survival test is to provide a method of 'picking winners'— or, rather, of diagnosing viable survivors among enterprises— which we are unable to replicate by any other means. Moreover, it also constitutes a method of stimulating poorly-performing businesses to re-organise.

Industrial policy, whether accelerative or decelerative in character, distorts the process of economic evolution in the market; indeed, that is its precise purpose. In doing so, however, it hampers the detection of viable businesses and the eradication of inefficiency. It thus threatens the ability of the market economy to cope with, adapt to, and take advantage of economic change. If pursued extensively, it is a danger to standards of living and economic progress.

In one guise or another, industrial policy has been around for a very long time. And, for just as long, economists have been exposing the fallacious nature of the arguments deployed to justify it. Henry Hazlitt's brilliant critique of them in 1947,[1] for example, drew heavily on the writings of Frédéric Bastiat almost a century earlier.

Why do governments indulge in activities which damage the process of economic evolution in the market? Why are they led to adopt policies which, if widely and persistently pursued, threaten long-term economic stagnation and decline? Such questions are the subject of the next Section.

---

[1] H. Hazlitt, *Economics in One Lesson*, Ernest Benn, London, 1947.

III. INDUSTRIAL POLICY AND THE POLITICAL MARKET

The implicit assumption of much orthodox writing on economic policy is that government is an exogenous agent acting in the public interest to apply necessary correctives to market processes and outcomes.

More recently, some economists, notably those associated with the Virginia School of public choice analysis in the USA, have developed the foundations of an economic analysis of politics.[1] This approach views government not as an exogenous force but as a self-interested party which responds to the structure of incentives it faces in the political arena. A related idea is that the political arena is in some respects analogous to a pecuniary market.

The nature of the political market

Specifically, we may conceive of citizens, and groups of citizens, as having preferences for different government policies. Those a citizen prefers will be 'demanded' by him in the political market; and his demand for a policy will, of course, be determined by the benefits and costs he perceives as flowing to himself. Conversely, politicians have an incentive to 'supply' those policies which appear to help them to retain political support and continue in office. The political market is the arena in which the forces of demand and supply for various government activities (taxing, subsidies, regulations, and so on) operate.

There are, of course, important differences between the operation of pecuniary and political markets. It is common in pecuniary markets, for example, for the terms of an exchange to be formally codified in the form of an explicit, written contract. The failure of one party to honour the terms of the agreed contract would render him liable to a breach-of-contract suit in civil law. The elector who votes for a politician

---

[1] For an introduction to the large literature on this subject, G. Tullock, *The Vote Motive*, Hobart Paperback 9, IEA, 1976.

or political party because of their promise to deliver a policy measure he or she desires has no such recourse if, after they are elected to power, they break that promise. The voter must wait for the next election.

In the pecuniary market, fraud—including fraudulent advertising—is punishable in the criminal courts, and breach of contract is actionable in the civil courts. Fraudulent or exaggerated political 'advertising'—policy promises which are not made good—is immune from legal redress. The 'contract' between voter and politician or party is unenforceable. To put it another way, while in constitutional theory the elected politician acts as the agent of his electors, they do not have the means of legally disciplining his behaviour if he fails to deliver the goods or services he has promised.[1] The 'agency relationship' between politician and elector is an extremely loose one—much looser than is typically found in pecuniary markets—and permits a wide degree of discretion to the agent (the politician).

For this and other reasons, the analogy between pecuniary and political markets must not be pushed too far.[2] Nevertheless, with this proviso, the concept of the political 'market' is useful.

Students of the economics of politics have devoted much attention to the demand for and supply of macro-economic policies. Some have argued that the operation of political demand and supply is likely to generate a political business cycle in which governments seek to attract political support by 'reflating' the economy just before general elections. Others have suggested that the working of demand and supply in the political market is likely, in the absence of a balanced-budget constraint on government, to lead to a persistent bias in government policy towards the creation of budget deficits.[3]

[1] In 1982 a certain Mrs Smith tried to sue the Prime Minister, Mrs Margaret Thatcher, under the law of tort. The plaintiff alleged that the Prime Minister's policies had caused her stress and mental cruelty; and, specifically, that they had caused her son to be unemployed for three years. The action, for £100,000, was struck out—the Prime Minister cannot be made legally liable for the alleged consequences of government policies, or for the laws passed by Parliament. ('Claim on Thatcher May Fail', *The Times*, 17 August 1982, p. 2.)

[2] This is discussed at more length in J. Burton and M. Hawkins, 'On Political Markets and Political Exchange', 1980, mimeo.

[3] J. M. Buchanan, J. Burton and R. E. Wagner, *The Consequences of Mr Keynes*, Hobart Paper 78, IEA, 1978, is one example.

Following the seminal work of Professor G. J. Stigler of the University of Chicago, growing attention has been given to the demand for and supply of micro-economic interventionist measures by government—and, specifically, to the demand for and supply of government *regulations*.[1] With the exception of an analysis of industrial policy by Professor C. K. Rowley of the University of Newcastle-upon-Tyne,[2] however, there has as yet been little consideration of industrial policy from the perspective of the economics of politics. The purpose of the present Section is to examine the formulation of industrial policy in the political market, drawing on the new perspectives offered by public choice analysis and, specifically, on the literature about the political economy of regulation.

Industrial policy under support-seeking government

The central tenet of public choice theory is that politicians, like actors in pecuniary markets, are self-interested agents—and not public-interest maximisers.

A standard assumption in the analysis of supply behaviour in pecuniary markets is that many actors are risk-averse, that is, they have a demand for security of employment. Translating this hypothesis to the political market, we presume that an incumbent government has a demand for security in office.

Political security requires the generation of various forms of political support. First, a government must have sufficient support from voters at election time to win. Secondly, it must have enough support within its own ranks (or within the ranks of a coalition of parties, if such exists) in the legislature to be able to enact policies and function as a government. Thirdly, it must have sufficient support from donors (in both time and money) to be able to advertise its 'products' (policies) in an appealing light, to carry out party administration, and to develop ideas for new 'products'.

These three forms of support can affect each other. Thus, while the generation of popularity with voters is clearly

---

[1] Professor Stigler's most important early works on this topic are collected in his *The Citizen and the State*, University of Chicago Press, Chicago, 1975. A brief outline of Stigler's analysis of regulation is contained in his *The Pleasures and Pains of Modern Capitalism*, Thirteenth Wincott Memorial Lecture, Occasional Paper 64, IEA, 1982.

[2] C. K. Rowley, 'Industrial Policy in the Mixed Economy', in E. Roll (ed.), *The Mixed Economy*, Macmillan, London, 1982, pp. 35-57.

critical at election time, it is not without significance between elections. For, other things equal, the higher a government's popularity, the lower is the probability of revolt within its own ranks in the legislature. Similarly, the more there is dissension within its own ranks, the more difficult it will be— other things equal—to attract donations since the return on these 'investments' expected by donors will be reduced.

Just as a business firm has a complex task to co-ordinate its marketing, production, personnel and financial operations into a coherent strategy for survival, so the political enterprise (party or presidential campaign) has a complex task to sustain the various and inter-related forms of political support necessary to preserve or enhance its prospects of political survival.

This analysis does not necessarily imply that governments are motivated *solely* by the desire for security of tenure, or that opposition parties are motivated *solely* by the desire to win power. As with actors in the pecuniary market, the variables in the utility function of the politician are liable to be numerous: security, status, income, ideology, altruism, and so on.

However, owing to the specific institutional characteristics of the political market (which derive from the very nature of government), the goal of winning or maintaining office is a necessary precondition for achieving other goals. In pecuniary markets, a business enterprise does not have to capture the entire market to make some profits, or afford its managers some status, or provide opportunities to indulge ideological or altruistic sentiments. In the political market, however, there is always one, and only one, supplier of government services at any point in time: the government is *the* government. Thus to achieve its other goals, a political party must first win power.

Providing subsidies through industrial policy is likely both to gain and lose support for a government. In enterprises which receive the subsidies, its popularity is likely to grow—especially if the subsidies avert bankruptcy. Moreover, backbench MPs in the constituencies where such enterprises are located are likely to be more supportive, or at least less critical, of the government. In this way, industrial policy may be deployed to generate support for the government.

The value of such support will depend, among other things, on how marginal the constituencies are in which subsidised enterprises are located. An increase in support in a constituency which is a 'safe' seat for the government is of little political

[51]

value. But an increase in popularity in a marginal constituency or one where a newly-arrived third-party candidate is likely to pose a considerable threat to the government party incumbent MP, is a different matter; gains here can be of critical importance. Thus enterprises in such marginal constituencies may find that subsidies are directed towards them with more readiness than towards others. There is evidence from a variety of sources that the allocation of industrial subsidies in Britain, in the form of regional aid, has been influenced by such factors.[1]

Hiding the costs of industrial policy

As has been seen, however, the provision of industrial subsidies to selected enterprises will generate a negative ripple effect in other parts of the economy which must bear the cost of financing them. Those so harmed, and their political representatives in the legislature, may consequently withdraw their support from the government.

Industrial policy thus requires a support-seeking government to make a delicate political calculus. It will prefer to allocate industrial subsidies in such a way as to yield a high ratio of support gained to support lost.

The volume of support lost by the application of an industrial policy is likely to be determined, among other things, by the magnitude and the transparency of the harm inflicted on other sectors of the economy. A lot of damage to the rest of the economy may lose little political support if it is barely detected by those who suffer; while a small amount may provoke a vociferous reaction if its harmful impact is highly transparent.

For illustrative purposes, let us assume that a large company is bailed out by government through the imposition of a special tax on another company. To give the example specific content, let us imagine that the subsidies paid to BL since 1975 had been financed not from general government revenue but by a special tax imposed on ICI. Such a policy might have gained, or at least retained, support for the government of the day in those constituencies in which BL plants (and those of their suppliers) are located. But both the size and the transparency of the enforced redistribution of resources from ICI to BL would doubt-

[1] In W. Grant, *The Political Economy of Industrial Policy*, Butterworth & Co., London, 1982, pp. 56-59.

Picking Losers . . . ?
JOHN BURTON

1. Loss-making and bankruptcy are as important as profits and corporate growth to the dynamism and evolutionary development of the market economy.
2. Winding-up a company does not mean the physical destruction of its assets; nor does it necessarily entail dismemberment of the company. It is a process of re-organisation, re-valuation, and change of ownership.
3. Industrial policy may be defined as government interference in the market process of economic evolution. Its main contemporary instrument is the injection of taxpayers' money into selected firms or industries.
4. Industrial policy can be classified as either 'accelerative' or 'decelerative'. The first aims to stimulate the birth rate of new business ventures, whereas the second seeks to reduce the death rate of senescent industries or enterprises.
5. Neither standard economic theory nor everyday experience offers any ground for the belief that politicians and bureaucrats are more alert in 'picking winners' of the future than private entrepreneurs motivated by opportunities for personal profit and possessed of specialised knowledge of business methods and markets.
6. The 'breathing space' provided to uncompetitive enterprises by decelerative industrial policy reduces the incentive for them to re-organise and shifts the costs of not adjusting on to others.
7. Whether financed by taxation, government borrowing or inflation, both decelerative and accelerative industrial policy have harmful direct and indirect effects on unsubsidised companies whose capacity to provide well-paid and secure jobs is thereby diminished.
8. The theory of public choice explains how the interaction of vote-seeking governments and subsidy-seeking producer groups encourages selective government intervention in industry and diverts managerial and trade union resources from productive uses to lobbying for government favours.
9. Under present fiscal arrangements, governments have a political incentive to subsidise firms in marginal constituencies and conceal the cost by spreading it among millions of taxpayers, consumers and savers in both current and future generations.
10. The appropriate role for government in its relations with industry is to avoid selective interventions which hamper adaptation to economic change. More positively, it should create a general environment in which business entrepreneurship can flourish on its own.

Hobart Paper 99 is published (price £2·00) by

THE INSTITUTE OF ECONOMIC AFFAIRS
2 Lord North Street, Westminster
London SW1P 3LB   Telephone: 01-799 3745

IEA PUBLICATIONS

Subscription Service

An annual subscription is the most convenient way to obtain our publications. Every title we produce in all our regular series will be sent to you immediately on publication and without further charge, representing a substantial saving.

Subscription rates*

Britain: £15·00 p.a. including postage.

£14·00 p.a. if paid by Banker's Order.

£10·00 p.a. teachers and students who pay *personally*.

Europe and South America: £20 or equivalent.

Other countries: Rates on application. In most countries subscriptions are handled by local agents.

*These rates are *not* available to companies or to institutions.

To: The Treasurer, Institute of Economic Affairs,
2 Lord North Street,
Westminster, London SW1P 3LB.

I should like to subscribe beginning....................................
I enclose a cheque/postal order for:

☐ £15·00

☐ Please send me a Banker's Order form

☐ Please send me an Invoice

☐ £10·00 [I am a teacher/student at.............................]

Name..

Address..

....

Signed.. Date..................

HP99

less have created a considerable loss of support, not to say a political storm, in those constituencies where ICI plants (and those of their suppliers) are located. Indeed, in this case the survival of BL might have been achieved only at the clear cost of bankrupting ICI. The obvious folly of such an industrial policy might have reduced public support for the government of the day in many enterprises and constituencies with no direct interest in the matter. Robbing Peter to pay Paul so nakedly would not be a sound choice for a support-seeking government.

If government were constrained by some written constitutional rule, or a binding constitutional convention, to finance all subsidies for a specific enterprise by a tax levied immediately on another enterprise, we could predict that the total volume of government support through industrial policy would be much smaller than it is under contemporary circumstances. (It would not, however, *necessarily* be zero. Despite the high visibility of the harm caused by industrial policy, and the general public opprobrium, the political value of increasing support in marginal constituencies might induce a government to allocate subsidies there and impose the cost on enterprises based in its own safe seats and seats safely held by opposition parties.)

Contemporary governments do not, however, operate industrial policy bound by such stringent constitutional rules or conventions. Under present fiscal arrangements, devices are available to government which markedly reduce the transparency of enforced redistributions. First, the visibility of the burden imposed on others can be reduced by spreading the tax costs among millions of taxpayers and by using several different forms of taxation. The wider the general tax base and the more numerous the sources of taxation, the lower will be the visibility of the costs imposed by industrial policy. And the larger the number of taxpayers who bear the costs of the policy, the more difficult it will be for them to organise a lobby to oppose a measure. In the extreme, the amount added to an individual taxpayer's bill may be so imperceptible that he is completely unaware he is bearing any cost at all.

The transparency of industrial policy as a redistributive device to gain political support may be further reduced, under present fiscal arrangements, by recourse to deficit financing. If the deficit of government is funded by creating money, the cost of industrial policy may emerge as inflation, and then only

[53]

after a lapse of time. Inflation operates as a tax on the holding of money balances, but is not widely perceived by the public as a form of taxation. If, on the other hand, the government deficit is funded by borrowing from the public, the cost of industrial policy falls on future taxpayers. It also raises the general level of interest rates in the short run, thereby retarding investment by numerous enterprises.

To summarise, the preceding analysis suggests that, under present fiscal arrangements, there is a political incentive for support-seeking governments to subsidise firms in marginal constituencies and spread the costs widely across the electorate.

Rent-seeking by collecting industrial subsidies

Just as government has a political incentive to provide subsidies to (certain) enterprises, so enterprises themselves have an incentive to acquire subsidies from government. The pursuit and acquisition of government subsidies may be seen as a form of rent-seeking.

By rent is meant not a return on property ownership (as in common parlance), but a return which is in excess of that required to keep a resource in its present use. Ownership of a unique resource which is in much demand but in fixed supply (such as Rod Stewart's or Placido Domingo's larynx) gives rise to rent in the sense employed by economists. But rent may arise from sources other than a natural limitation of supply; it may be generated artificially. The term 'rent-seeking' has been coined by economists to describe the creation of rent by deliberate contrivance.[1]

One avenue of rent-seeking which economists have long analysed is the device of market closure or capture. The most common form is by means of collusion among sellers to effect a co-ordinated reduction in supply or the enforcement of a uniform higher price. The rent created thereby is known as 'monopoly rent'.

While the monopoly rent generated by collusion, cartelisation, and restrictive practices has been the form of rent-seeking most analysed by economists, it is not in practice the most important and enduring. This is so because the market economy contains a process which subjects all rent-seeking

---

[1] For a fuller examination of the concept and its applications, J. M. Buchanan, R. D. Tollison, and G. Tullock (eds.), *Toward a Theory of the Rent-seeking Society*, Texas A&M University Press, College Station, 1980.

activities to forces of erosion. Its essence is that the attempt by any group to rig the market itself generates incentives for others to undermine it. Other entrepreneurs, outside the cartel, have a direct incentive to undercut the prices that are rigged. Even the members of the cartel have a financial incentive to 'chisel', that is, to declare that they are selling at the cartel-established price whilst selling below it in practice. And consumers have an interest in rewarding the cartel-breakers by giving them their custom.

Thus, unless the state—or an institution, such as the Mafia, with the same powers to coerce as the state—prevents this 'market escape' process from functioning, or unless the cartel owns a completely unique resource (in which case the rent is natural), the very operation of a cartel in a market economy sets off forces which will eventually erode it. Monopoly rent-seeking in a market economy is a precarious business.

Another, and more enduring, form of rent creation is through the powers of government. Here, the government is induced to extract rent for the benefit of selected groups by promises of votes, donations to campaign funds, and/or bribes. The inducement may also take the form of a threat to punish the government in some way (by delivering votes to an opposing party, for example).

The variety of methods by which government can create rent for an enterprise is large. A straightforward approach is to grant it a state-enforced monopoly by prohibiting competition against the enterprise's products. This method was common during the mercantilist era and is again widespread today—many nationalised industries in Britain enjoy a statutory monopoly. A more subtle method is for government to introduce regulations, such as licensing laws and agencies, which prevent entry into an industry. This technique is more prevalent in the United States, but is by no means rare in Britain.[1] A further method is to restrict imports through the imposition of tariffs or quotas on foreign supplies to the domestic market.[2] Since the General Agreement on Tariffs and

---

[1] The seminal analysis of rent-seeking *via* regulation, by Professor G. J. Stigler, is referred to above, p. 50, note 1.

[2] R. E. Baldwin, 'The Political Economy of Protectionism', in J. N. Bhagwati (ed.), *Import Competition and Response*, University of Chicago Press, 1982, pp. 263-86; and W. A. Brock and S. P. Magee, 'The Economics of Special Interest Politics: The Case of the Tariff', *American Economic Review Papers and Proceedings*, Vol. 68, May 1978, pp. 69-90.

Trade (GATT) has, for the most part, succeeded in outlawing quotas and discriminatory tariffs in the industrialised world during the post-war era, it is not surprising that enterprises have sought government-created rent by other devices—notably subsidies—over this period.

Lobbying for subsidies is conducted most effectively by those groups best organised to do it. Large enterprises tend to be more proficient at lobbying than small ones; and old industries more proficient than young ones. The existence of a strong trade union organisation within an industry is a factor which reinforces the effectiveness of lobbying, as well as spreading its cost.

For an enterprise in imminent danger of bankruptcy, the opportunity cost of lobbying is much lower than for a successful, profit-making firm. For the latter, it means diverting managerial talent which is profitably employed in organising the production of goods or services into the business of manipulating and cajoling politicians and bureaucrats. A loss-making company, on the other hand, has no profits to forego by allocating the time and effort of its executives to the task of wheedling money out of government.

Rent-seeking is a negative-sum 'game'

Rent-seeking through the medium of government thus represents at best a zero-sum game—a purely redistributive activity. It is, however, more likely to turn into a negative-sum game, resulting in a net loss of output for society. This is so because the assignment of special privileges by government—whether subsidies, a privileged monopoly, tariff protection, or whatever—will tend to encourage others to play the same game. It encourages other businesses to specialise in adroit political lobbying. Consequently, time and effort which were previously devoted to creating real wealth in competitive markets for goods and services are diverted into unproductive rent-seeking in the political market.[1]

Lessons from home and abroad

Two examples—from the UK and Israel—will serve to illus-

[1] This cost, associated with the diversion of economic effort into lobbying for transfers enforced by government, and into lobbying to offset them, is known as the 'Tullock welfare loss' of government transfers, after the seminal treatment in G. Tullock, 'The Cost of Transfers', *Kyklos*, 4, December 1971, pp. 629-43.

trate how industrial subsidies stimulate efforts by other firms to seek to acquire rent by the same means.

Shortly after taking office in May 1979, the (then) Secretary of State for Industry, Sir Keith Joseph, charged the British Steel Corporation (BSC) with the task of breaking even during the financial year of 1980-81. In the event, it incurred a net loss of £660 million in that year. In early 1981 a government 'reconstruction' of BSC's finances was announced, entailing the writing-off of no less than £3,550 million of public money owed by the Corporation. The Government also announced that it would provide the Corporation with a further £730 million in 1981-82. This glowing example of successful rent-seeking in the political market by BSC led the British Independent Steel Producers Association to step up the volume of its own lobbying. In 1981, it argued that its member firms were:

'. . . currently suffering indirectly the adverse effects of all that Government has done, and is still doing, to rescue BSC. The Secretary of State and his colleagues have been clearly warned over recent months that they are in imminent danger of being the instruments of the collapse of the private sector . . .'[1]

This lobbying did not cause the Government to reduce the large subsidies given to the BSC. Instead, after 1980-81, it started to give new financial assistance to the independent steelmakers too.

A study of the growth of industrial subsidies in Israel, by Professor Nathan Finger, provides a second example of how subsidies proliferate.[2] Indeed, Israel is an almost perfect model of the phenomenon; as early as 1967, the total of government grants and loans to industry there outstripped private equity investment as a source of finance for industry.

Professor Finger's study documents how the subsidisation of some sectors of Israeli industry led other firms to intensify their efforts to acquire similar rent. Indeed, it eventually spawned an entire species of what he describes as 'subsidy-maximising firms'. These enterprises came to depend on the manipulation of subsidy systems for a major portion (sometimes the bulk) of their income.

[1] Industry and Trade Committee, Fourth Report, *Effects of BSC's Corporate Plan; Minutes of Evidence and Appendices*, HMSO, London, HC 336-II, 1981, p. 125.

[2] N. Finger, *The Impact of Government Subsidies on Industrial Management: The Israeli Experience*, Praeger, New York, 1974.

From Israel's subsidy morass there emerged a new type of management executive and consultant who specialised in understanding the vast array of subsidies available to industry and how to extract them successfully from government. Many such executives and consultants were ex-officials of the government departments and agencies responsible for disbursing industrial subsidies.

A similar development has evidently been taking place in the British economy over the post-war period, most notably during the 1970s.[1] Nor did the change of government in May 1979 alter the upward trajectory of the growth of industrial subsidies. Although the new Conservative Government originally announced its intention to reduce the budget of the Department of Industry after 1980-81, quite the reverse happened:

'. . . the projected figures for 1981-2 (at 1980 survey prices) increased to £1,554 million, the highest level since 1975-76, and representing a real increase of forty-two per cent on 1979-80 and twenty-three per cent on 1980-81'.[2]

These figures do not take account fully of the growth of subsidies, notably in 1981, to 'big loser' nationalised enterprises such as the National Coal Board and British Rail.[3]

The British industrial subsidy morass has induced the same phenomenon as in Israel of rising business investment in the activity of lobbying government. During the 1970s in particular, many large British firms established 'government relations departments' with executives of high calibre.[4] They also started to make much use of bought-in advice from Parliamentary consultants. Predictably, consultants who specialise in advising about the acquisition of industrial grants have now begun to appear in the UK.[5]

The interests of the industrial policy bureaucracy

The preceding analysis has shown how the interaction of support-seeking government and rent-seeking producer groups

---

[1] For fuller details, J. Burton, *The Job Support Machine: A Critique of the Subsidy Morass*, Centre for Policy Studies, London, 1979.

[2] W. Grant, *op. cit.*, p. 97.

[3] The Thatcher Government's industrial policy of so-called 'constructive intervention' is considered further in Section IV.

[4] W. Grant, *op. cit.*, p. 44.

[5] For example, 'Advice on Getting Grants', *The Observer*, 5 February 1978, p. 15.

operating in the political market is likely to lead, at least under current constitutional arrangements, to the emergence of industrial policy. And industrial policy has to be administered. It thus gives rise to a bureaucracy of agencies, departments, inter-departmental groupings and 'quangos' whose business is to apply, monitor, administer and develop the policy.

The administrative structures associated with industrial policy can be termed the industrial policy bureaucracy.[1] In practice, industrial policy in most countries is not centralised in one monolithic bureaucracy; it is administered by a web of inter-connected agencies, commissions, councils, and so on. In the UK, for example, the government departments which are involved in aspects of industrial policy include not only the Department of Trade and Industry, but also the Treasury, the Scottish and Welsh Offices (which administer discretionary regional aid under the 1972 Industry Act), the Department of Energy (the sponsoring ministry for the coal and electricity industries), the Department of Transport (with responsibility for British Rail, among other things), the Department of Commerce in Northern Ireland, and the Scottish Economic Planning Department (the economic policy arm of the Scottish Office). Linked to these departments is a plethora of agencies and boards, such as the nine Research Requirements Boards set up by the Department of Industry (as it then was), industrial research establishments such as the National Engineering Laboratory, the Advisory Council for Applied Research and Development, the Small Firms Service, the Scottish and Welsh Development Agencies, the National Economic Development Council (under which some 39 major 'sector working parties' are also constituted), the Council for Small Industries in Rural Areas, the Development Board for Rural Wales, the Highlands and Islands Development Board, the English Industrial Estates Corporation, the British Technology Group (formed by the merger of the former National Enterprise Board and the National Research Development Corporation), the Invest in Britain Bureau, the Development Corporation for Wales, the Development Commission, the Locate in Scotland Bureau, and yet others.

[1] W. Grant, *op. cit.*, Ch. II, uses the term 'industrial policy community' to describe both the agencies administering industrial policy and the personnel located in enterprises and unions whose job it is to lobby for subsidies and other favours provided by government.

The above list, which is by no means complete,[1] represents a very considerable bureaucratic structure, which has mushroomed over recent decades. This large administrative overhead constitutes a further cost imposed on the economy by industrial policy. The huge resources it pre-empts could otherwise be employed to produce valued goods and services in the market economy.

Very often the interests of the multifarious parts of this industrial policy empire conflict. If the Scottish Development Agency is successful in luring a company to Scotland with loans and grants, it is often at the expense of some other location for which another agency is responsible. Of the 225 companies which have settled in Warrington New Town over the last 10 years, for example, 79 were re-locations, 30 of them from depressed areas such as Merseyside (which was a major factor in the latter's decision to set up its own development corporation with funds to lure industry back!).[2] This is another aspect of the counter-productive nature of industrial policy, which adds to the waste of the British economy's resources.

Although the particular interests the industrial policy bureaucracy purports to serve frequently find themselves in conflict with one another, the bureaucracy's own interest is in preserving (and enlarging) its size and functions. It constitutes a powerful and sophisticated lobby for industrial policy *within* the apparatus of government.

The international political economy of industrial policy

Economic policy analysis traditionally drew a distinction between 'domestic' and 'international' policies, according to the policy instrument employed. Thus tariffs, quotas, and other types of measures taking effect at the borders of a country were classified as international; all others were domestic. However,

---

[1] An important feature of industrial subsidisation in Britain over recent years has been its growth at the regional and even council level. While regional promotion has for long been extensive in Wales and Scotland, regional development agencies have sprouted in England also (e.g., the Merseyside Development Corporation; the Devon and Cornwall Bureau). Twenty New Town Development Corporations also promote the location of industry in and around them. And local authorities are allowed the equivalent of a 2p rate for this purpose—the most recent product of such funding being the West Midlands Enterprise Board which is supported by £7·5 million of ratepayers' money.

[2] For further details of this and other such cases, C. Tighe, 'Revealed: The £750m Tug-of-Work', *Sunday Times*, 'Business News', 21 February 1982, p. 60.

the growth of industrial policy (and other forms of government intervention) in the post-war context of increasing economic interdependence between countries has greatly eroded the relevance of the distinction.[1] In an interdependent world economy, domestic industrial policy often has wide-ranging trade effects on industry and employment prospects in other countries and on the location decisions of internationally mobile firms.

'Domestic' industrial policy also has international *political* ramifications. Producers who are harmed by other countries' industrial policies are given a direct incentive to lobby their own governments for protection against subsidised imports—in the form of either matching subsidies or countervailing duties or quotas. Domestic industrial policy thus has the international political effect of promoting international imitation.

That this development has been growing apace in the world economy over recent decades is now beyond question. The Director of Economic Research and Analysis of the GATT Secretariat, Jan Tumlir, has summarised what has been happening thus:

'The international trading system is cumulating difficulties. The proportion of transactions conducted under all kinds of non-tariff restraint [of trade] has been growing. It has increased by at least five percentage points between 1974 and 1980 . . . According to various estimates, this proportion is now between 40 and 48 per cent of world trade.

'. . . Important constituent elements of the systems of industrial protection as they have emerged since around 1970 are public subsidies . . . With the exception of the United States, the level of such subsidies in relation to gross domestic product was everywhere higher in 1979 than in 1970 (and in 1970 the level of subsidies was at least triple the level of 1955).'[2]

Conclusion

The interaction of vote-seeking government and rent-seeking producer groups has resulted in the enormous growth of industrial policy over the post-war period. The international

---

[1] R. Blackhurst, 'The Twilight of Domestic Economic Policies', *The World Economy*, Vol. 4, No. 4, December 1981, pp. 357-74.

[2] J. Tumlir, 'International Economic Order—Can the Trend be Reversed?', *The World Economy*, Vol. 5, No. 1, March 1982, pp. 29-30.

consequences of this development now pose a major threat to world trade and to the preservation of an open international economic order.

Industrial policy imposes three main sets of costs. First, it damages the process of economic evolution. Secondly, it burdens healthy parts of the economy by delayed adjustments elsewhere. Thirdly, it diverts money and management skills from the task of production to the scramble for subsidies and other government favours.

IV. THE RESTORATION OF ECONOMIC EVOLUTION?

What measures ought to be adopted to revitalise the market process of economic evolution, the damaged mainspring of economic progress? And what do they imply for government economic policy towards industry? Answering these questions, albeit tentatively, is the object of this Section. First, however, we will briefly review recent changes in British industrial policy in order to assess the extent to which they represent a shift towards the restoration of economic evolution.

Constructive industrial policy: the right approach?

Before coming to office in 1979, the Conservative Party's economic policy team published its general economic and industrial strategy.[1] This document had, however, little of substance to say about the actual content of industrial policy under a future Conservative government. The accompanying rhetoric of Mrs Thatcher and her colleagues at that time suggested a more substantive attempt would be made to disengage government from industry than the (aborted) effort of the Heath Government between 1970 and 1974.

In 1980, Conservative ministers began to describe the new Government's strategy towards industry as 'constructive industrial policy' and/or 'constructive intervention'. What has been its content, and does it represent a real commitment towards the abandonment of accelerative and decelerative industrial policies?

It is, first, necessary to reiterate that the sums of taxpayer finance allocated to industrial policy have not been reduced under the aegis of 'constructive intervention'.[2] On the contrary, they have grown very considerably in nominal (money) terms. Specifically, the very large subsidies allocated to ailing public sector enterprises—such as British Leyland, British Steel

---

[1] A. Maude *et al.*, *The Right Approach to the Economy*, Conservative Central Office, London, 1977.

[2] J. Burton, 'The Thatcher Experiment—A Requiem?', *Journal of Labor Research*, August 1981, Research Monograph 1, pp. 23-26.

Corporation, British Shipbuilders, British Aerospace and British Rail—were a major factor in boosting total government spending above its target in 1980-81. (Total spending by the Department of Industry stood at £980 million in 1977-78; by 1981-82 it had risen to £1,988 million.)

While the volume of industrial subsidies has grown under 'constructive industrial policy', however, there has been some alteration in its composition for the following reasons. First, the geographical size of the Assisted Areas was considerably pared down between 1979 and 1982.[1] Secondly, the Selective Investment Scheme was terminated in 1979 (although outstanding applications were processed, under revised criteria). And thirdly, more emphasis has been placed on accelerative industrial policy; larger sums have been allocated to the stimulation of small businesses (e.g. the bank loan guarantee scheme for small businesses announced in the 1981 Budget, the business expansion scheme, the venture capital scheme, and the share buy-back legislation). Moreover, there has been considerable growth—representing *82 per cent* in real terms between 1979 and 1981-82—in the allocation of taxpayer finance to general R and D expenditures, including a doubling of the outlays on micro-electronics. More taxpayer funds have also been devoted to introducing new technology into the production processes of older industries (under the Product and Process Development Scheme), and to encouraging research in information technology.

In summary, the thrust of 'constructive industrial policy' does not represent a move towards the restoration of economic evolution. Rather, it represents a 'touch on the tiller' in the application of industrial policy, specifically in a more accelerative direction.

A *caveat* is necessary in view of the Government's efforts to privatise some state-owned enterprises and agencies which have injected a more positive element into the revitalisation of economic evolution. Even here, however, the selling-off of assets has frequently been only partial, with the government retaining around 50 per cent of the enterprises.[2]

[1] *Regional Industrial Policy Changes, July 1979 to August 1982*, Department of Industry, London, February 1981.

[2] For a more detailed discussion of the industrial policy of the 1979-83 Government, W. Grant, *The Political Economy of Industrial Policy*, Butterworth & Co., London, 1982, pp. 78-100.

Industrial policy as amelioration of macro-economic policy

Another feature of contemporary British industrial policy is that, despite the shift in emphasis towards (hopefully) 'sun*rise*' industries[1] and small firms, the bulk of subsidies continues to go to 'sun*set*' industries. It has been estimated that, in 1980-81, they received some 60 to 70 per cent of all government aid to industry.[2]

One reason for this continuing bias of industrial policy is that the Cabinet has apparently thought it necessary, for political reasons, to be seen to be mitigating the short-term unemployment effects of its adherence to a tighter monetary/fiscal policy stance by 'generous' industrial policy measures.[3] Unfortunately, this posture overlooks the long-run benefits which economic natural selection confers on the economy. As Professor Richard C. Stapleton has argued:

'. . . the destruction of unadaptable industry [even] in a deep recession can be a major benefit, if not an essential pre-requisite, for change'.[4]

There is a danger that such an industrial policy will partly negate the benefits of macro-economic policy.[5] To that extent, the present Government's industrial policy may be said to be at cross-purposes with its Medium-Term Financial Strategy.

PROPOSALS FOR REFORM

If constructive industrial policy does not signify a move to restore economic evolution, what measures *would*? Six are proposed in what follows.

[1] 'Constructive' industrial policy has been defined by Mrs Thatcher as 'stimulating industries which do have a future, rather than shoring up lost causes; helping to create tomorrow's world rather than to preserve yesterday's'; quoted in J. Elliott, 'Sir Keith Looks for Winners', *Financial Times*, 6 January 1981.

[2] Statement by the Director-General of the National Economic Development Office, *Financial Times*, 8 April 1981.

[3] 'Mrs Thatcher's resolve not to prop up lame ducks has had to be subdued under the Cabinet's majority view against action which would bring heavy redundancies . . .'. (James Wightman, 'Resolve on Lame Duck Firms Subdued by Cabinet', *Daily Telegraph*, 2 February 1981, p. 2.)

[4] R. C. Stapleton, 'Why Recession Benefits Britain', *Journal of Economic Affairs*, Vol. 2, No. 1, October 1981, p. 8 (original in italics).

[5] W. M. Corden, 'Relationships between Macro-economic and Industrial Policies', *The World Economy*, Vol. 3, No. 2, September 1980, pp. 167-84.

(i) *Policy to enhance the general environment of industry*

Restoring economic prosperity in the UK—as elsewhere—will require the abandonment of selective industrial policy. More reliance will have to be placed on economic evolution in the market as the guide to economic change and development. This does not, however, imply that government must adopt a neutral role towards industry. As Professor Assar Lindbeck has argued, it would mean that

'. . . the task of government would then be to try to create an economic, social, and political environment that is conducive to efficiency and new initiatives'.[1]

The agenda for these general actions should include an extensive de-regulation of product and labour markets, the removal of government-imposed entry barriers to industries and occupations, and a considerable reduction in both the rates and progressiveness of taxation.[2] Moreover, it requires that government provision of public goods must become more *efficient*. Inefficiency in the non-market sector of the economy makes for a heavier burden on the market sector and thus hampers its performance.

Although Japan is often cited as having 'the most consistent and complete system of industrial policy',[3] this impression is mistaken. As two Japanese economists have stressed:

'. . . Japanese industrial policy is not confined within the concept usually held in the industrialised countries . . . Indeed [Japanese] industrial policy is sometimes understood as competition-maintaining policy . . . it rarely aims to develop or redress particular sectors but is, rather, a *general* system of policies aimed at industrial development and promotion.'[4]

Britain's leading expert on the Japanese economy until his death in 1982, Professor G. C. Allen, wrote:

'It is probable that the post-war [Japanese] government's chief

[1] A. Lindbeck, 'Industrial Policy as an Issue of the Economic Environment', *The World Economy*, Vol. 4, No. 4, December 1981, p. 396.

[2] Specific proposals to enhance the environment of industry are examined in A. Lindbeck, *ibid.*, and in V. Curzon-Price, 'Alternatives to Delayed Structural Adjustment in Workshop Europe', *The World Economy*, Vol. 3, No. 2, September 1980, pp. 205-16.

[3] J. Pinder, 'Industrial Policy and the International Economy', in J. Pinder (ed.), *National Industrial Strategies and the World Economy*, Allanheld, Osmun and Co., Totowa, N.J., 1982, p. 265.

[4] T. Hosomi and A. Okumura, 'Japanese Industrial Policy', in J. Pinder (ed.), *ibid.*, p. 123 (italics added).

contribution to economic progress was its provision of a congenial environment for innovators.'[1]

In short, Japanese 'industrial policy' comprises general measures to enhance the environment of industry rather than selective interventions on the contemporary European model. The economy of Japan is highly competitive and its public sector is very small in terms of employment and as a proportion of GNP compared with other industrialised countries.

A policy stance of enhancing the environment of industry by general measures (such as constraining the size of the non-market sector) must be adopted if Western countries are to match the widely-admired economic success of Japan in recent decades. To seek to imitate Japan's record by government intervention in economic evolution is based on a serious misunderstanding of that country's 'industrial policy' and will lead inexorably in the opposite economic direction to that desired.

In this context, some elements of the British Government's small firms policy are to be commended, in that they are aimed more at enhancing the general environment for small business than at selecting supposed winners. Other aspects of its industrial policy are less commendable, if not undesirable, on this criterion. One example is the creation of enterprise zones, the first 11 of which were established in 1980, and a further 13 more recently. It may be argued that this selective assistance distorts the property market and locational decisions rather than providing a stimulus to economic growth.[2]

A main barrier to enhancing the environment for industry lies in the workings of the political market. Section III described how the interaction of vote-seeking governments and rent-seeking producer groups encourages selective government intervention in industry which damages economic evolution and diverts resources away from productive use towards the jockeying for government subsidies and other favours. Moreover, the workings of domestic political markets also have international consequences which are currently threatening world trade and international specialisation according to comparative

---

[1] G. C. Allen, *How Japan Competes*, Hobart Paper 81, IEA, 1978, p. 30.

[2] For further discussion, R. Botham and G. Lloyd, 'The Political Economy o Enterprise Zones', *National Westminster Bank Quarterly Review*, May 1983, pp. 24-32. The theory of enterprise zone policy is explored in S. M. Butler, *Enterprise Zones*, Critical Issues Series, Heritage Foundation, Washington DC, 1980.

efficiency. Thus, effective policies to improve the environment for industry will require reforms in both domestic political markets and international trading agreements.

(ii) *Treatment of small business as a general experimental zone*

A policy of enhancing the environment of industry by general de-regulation would come up against two major obstacles. Both would arise from the way in which the political market normally operates. First, general de-regulation would require a 'big bang approach' to the withdrawal of government from industrial intervention. While this approach was tried—and, indeed, *worked* politically and economically—in Ludwig Erhard's 'bonfire of controls' experiment in the Germany of 1950, the cumbersome nature of modern democratic government militates against its adoption today. Secondly, since many producer groups (industries, firms, unions) gain from selective regulation,[1] the more the de-regulation attempted, the louder would be the outcry from various lobbying groups.[2]

The political problem, therefore, is how to extend the scope for natural economic evolution in the economy without confronting timid government with a wall of lobbying opposition. One practical suggestion is to treat all small businesses (of, say, up to 100 employees) as a 'general experimental zone' of the economy. The principal feature of this zone would be that, within it, regulations and taxation were reduced to zero or the barest minimum.[3]

The concept of small business as a general experimental zone has a number of attractions. First, it would avoid the geographical (and related) distortions introduced by present-day enterprise zones. Secondly, on evidence from the United States, small business is very much more innovative than large for each dollar of R & D expenditure, and has provided the bulk of new private-sector jobs there since 1969.[4] Thirdly, it would

---

[1] G. J. Stigler, *The Pleasures and Pains of Modern Capitalism, op. cit.*

[2] This point has been made by H. Grubel, *Free Market Zones,* The Fraser Institute, Vancouver, 1983.

[3] Practical suggestions for the de-regulation of a small business zone are in M. Pirie, 'Regulations *vs.* the Portable Enterprise Zone', in E. Butler (ed.), *The Real Causes of Unemployment,* Adam Smith Institute, London, 1983, pp. 83-91.

[4] For fuller discussion, J. Burton, 'Job Saving and Creation by Industrial and Manpower Policies', in E. Butler (ed.), *ibid.*, pp. 10-25.

extend the scope for open economic evolution while not requiring a 'big bang approach' to de-regulation.

The dynamism of small firms in Italy, where those with fewer than 20 employees are exempt from many official regulations, indicates the potential for economic evolution with a de-regulated small business sector.

(iii) *The role of a balanced budget rule*

There is a strong bias in democratic political markets towards deficit financing of government expenditure.[1] Fundamentally, this arises because it is a more effective way of hiding the costs of government spending than is financing by taxation. Tax finance directly reduces the resources of those who are required to pay the taxes, and such citizens constitute a strong political lobby against the erosion of their disposable wealth by government. Deficit financing, on the other hand, conceals and postpones the costs of government expenditure, a process which, because it is ill-understood, provokes less resentment from those who ultimately have to meet the bill. Deficit financing is thus a very attractive device for concentrating the benefits and diffusing the costs of government activities.

Predictably, ever since the Keynesian revolution sanctified a persistent discrepancy between government spending and tax finance, governments have resorted more and more to the political tactic of winning support by spending more than they raise in taxation. The emergence of contemporary industrial policy is to be understood as part of that process, given also the international political constraints in the post-war era on tariff discrimination against foreign competition.

By making its costs more explicit to taxpayers, a balanced-budget constraint on government spending would do much to remove this bias in the present fiscal system. A fundamental drawback of this proposal, however, is that the UK does not have a written constitution, and therefore has no way of amending it by due constitutional process (as in the United States). The British constitution, such as it is, is largely a matter of 'conventions' accepted by Parliament. And since Parliament is effectively dominated by the House of Commons, and the latter by the majority party, it is no exaggeration to

[1] J. M. Buchanan, J. Burton and R. M. Wagner, *op. cit.*

say that the content of the British constitution is partly at the mercy of the Prime Minister of the day.

The introduction of an effective balanced-budget constitutional rule in the UK would thus require a constitutional revolution to include the adoption of a written constitution. The arguments for so fundamental a reform are, indeed, much wider than the mere containment of costly industrial policies. They go to the roots of the question whether contemporary democracy should be constitutional or a form of 'elective tyranny'.[1]

(iv) *Re-training vouchers/tax credits*

Economic change produces losers as well as gainers. People working in obsolescent industries and firms discover that it threatens their livelihood and may considerably reduce the value of the human capital they have invested in specific forms of training. They therefore have an incentive to lobby for government measures designed to prevent or postpone change.

Government vouchers to cover the cost of re-training would be a means of buying out the resistance of these vested producer-group interests. Individuals who lost their jobs would be given a voucher entitling them to training in an enterprise (including educational enterprises) which accepted the voucher, the cost of which would be borne by the taxpayer. The enterprise would encash the voucher at an appropriate government agency. The value of a voucher might be related to the number of years of service in the previous employment (and thus, very roughly, to the value of the human capital investment which had to be written off).

An objection to such a scheme is that some individuals might have valid reasons for preferring the cash itself—to start a business of their own, for example. For this reason, it would be advisable to incorporate a means of enabling a displaced employee to cash his re-training voucher directly, provided the cash was to be used exclusively to create a new business.

Whereas industrial policy subsidises particular enterprises and industries, thus damaging the process of economic evolution, re-training vouchers would subsidise *individuals* adversely affected by economic change. Moreover, while industrial subsidies create an incentive for enterprises and unions to lobby

---

[1] Further discussion of these important issues is in Lord Hailsham, *The Dilemma of Democracy: Diagnosis and Prescription*, Collins, London, 1978.

for government measures to prevent economic change, a system of re-training vouchers would create an incentive for individuals to accept it.

An alternative to re-training vouchers, which is based on similar lines of reasoning, is the proposal by the 'Wednesday Group' in the United States that companies which teach new skills to redundant workers should be given tax credits to set against their expenditure on training.

A major advantage of both schemes is that they do not rely on government to forecast the direction of economic evolution. Workers and firms would be making their own—varied—assessments of the direction of economic evolution.

(v) *Disciplining loss-making government enterprises*

The most serious damage to the process of economic evolution is caused by certain large, loss-making, state-owned enterprises. The discipline of corporate bankruptcy has for them been virtually suspended, and the taxpayer has been dragooned into becoming an unlimited liability guarantor of all their losses. Moreover, the costs of their activities are hidden from the taxpayer because the losses are funded from general taxation. Furthermore, their losses are often so huge that the enterprises are difficult—but not necessarily impossible[1]—to privatise.

The solution lies in *giving away* the ownership rights in these enterprises to the general public. After all, they are often (and quite inaccurately) described as 'publicly-owned'. In reality, the public does not own them: they are owned by the state and controlled by government. Taxpayers at present have no ownership *rights* in them at all; they have merely the *obligation*, enforced through the tax system, to fund their losses. Distributing the ownership rights to all electors would establish true public ownership.

One way of doing this has been suggested by Professor Milton Friedman.[2] His idea is to create a mutual fund comprising the equity of a number of (presently) state-owned enterprises, both profitable and loss-making. The public would then be able to discipline the management of the enterprises by determining the price of the mutual's shares on the stock market.

Another method would be to distribute to electors the shares

[1] See the discussion on this matter in Section II, pp. 41-42.

[2] M. Friedman, *From Galbraith to Economic Freedom*, Occasional Paper 49, IEA, 1977, pp. 51-53.

in individual loss-making state enterprises and stipulate that, for a period of, say, five years, these ownership rights would carry unlimited liability—after when they would enjoy limited liability. If an enterprise continued to make losses, each owner would discover the costs of its inefficiency in the form of a direct billing arrangement. Each would have a direct incentive to discipline the incumbent management through his or her voting rights in the corporation. It can be predicted that the re-organisation of such an enterprise would take place at a very much faster pace than at present. Currently, electors have no direct means of influencing the performance of state-owned corporations, and do not even know how much tax they pay to subsidise their losses.[1]

(vi) *Escaping the international repercussions of industrial policy*

In the integrated world economy of the post-war era, industrial policy pursued for domestic political purposes wreaks economic damage on enterprises in other countries, provoking demands in the latter for countervailing subsidies and other protective measures. In thus breeding retaliation, industrial policy under-mines the GATT system and curbs the flows of international trade.

If the downward spiral of distortion and retaliation is to be arrested, there must be an international agreement to disarm on non-tariff barriers to trade. Though this is a lengthy and technical matter,[2] the general substance of such an agreement may be briefly outlined. What is required is a prohibition on certain forms of industrial policy which distort trade—or, at the very least, a time limit on their use. And the agreement must have teeth; there must be enforceable penalties for transgression. Finally, there must be a workable arbitration procedure to resolve disputes.

The failure of the Geneva ministerial conference of the GATT in November 1982 to make tangible progress on these

---

[1] An alternative scheme proposing tax remissions for those who save and invest in de-nationalised stocks is proposed by R. Lewis, 'How to Denationalise', in R. Boyson (ed.), *Goodbye to Nationalisation*, Churchill Press, 1971, pp. 80-90.

[2] Detailed discussions are provided by G. Curzon and V. Curzon, *Global Assault on Non-Tariff Trade Barriers* (1972); H. B. Malmgren, *International Order for Public Subsidies* (1977); and G. Denton and S. O'Cleireacain, *Subsidy Issues in International Commerce* (1972), all published by the Trade Policy Research Centre, London.

[72]

issues is a sombre reminder that the negotiation of international agreements is no easy task. Since, however, the alternative is the prospect of a trade war,[1] achieving such an agreement remains an urgent international responsibility.

On economic evolution and economic security: a general conclusion

Economic evolution in the market is the process whereby economic progress is achieved. Government intervention in that process jeopardises economic progress.

The superficial attraction of decelerative industrial policy is that it appears to offer more economic security to those who are adversely affected by economic change and progress. Faced with a choice between progress and security, many might well opt for the latter.

But this choice is illusory. Decelerative industrial policy cannot provide general security. All that it can do is to *shift the costs* of not adjusting from particular companies or industries to the rest of the economy, whose capacity to provide security is thereby reduced. More security is given to the non-adjusting sector only by creating insecurity elsewhere. And if it is applied on a sufficiently grand scale, decelerative industrial policy can afford security to no-one because there is precious little security in economic stagnation and industrial sclerosis.

This message is not new,[2] but it apparently requires continuous repetition. Britain's post-war history of escalating attempts to shore up declining industries by government intervention has been an important factor in its relative economic decline. Not only has decelerative policy failed to provide economic security; it has been in considerable measure responsible for the economic stagnation. Over the period 1945 to 1979, government support of the nationalised industries alone was of the order of £31·6 billion (at 1979 survey prices).[3] Where

[1] K. Richardson and R. Righter, 'Trade War Looms after GATT Flop', *Sunday Times,* 28 November 1982, p. 1.

[2] 'Fifty years ago Professor A. G. B. Fisher [in his book entitled *The Clash of Progress and Security*] pointed out, with great prescience, that the single-minded pursuit of security at the expense of progress would threaten to sacrifice both progress and security'. (R. Harris, *The End of Government . . .?*, Occasional Paper 58, IEA, 1980, p. 56.)

[3] This estimate is contained in information supplied by the Government in response to questions tabled in the House of Lords by Lord Harris of High Cross on 6 October and 4 November 1980.

[73]

is the economic security for the British worker in the 1980s which this money supposedly bought? These vast subventions have not only retarded economic progress; they have seriously diminished general economic security. Indeed, by storing up a backlog of adjustment, they have immensely magnified the difficulties Britain faces today.

Accelerative industrial policy appears at first sight to be a more constructive response to the presumed clash between progress and security. It purports to provide more security in the future by accelerating the progress of certain new firms, new technologies and new industries. Being 'forward-looking' in its approach, it seems to promise economic progress. This also is an illusion, because governments do not possess the information to pick the 'winners' of the future. The sorry financial history of the Concorde supersonic jetliner is a telling example of the more general problem. Moreover, accelerative industrial policy, no less than the decelerative variety, imposes burdens on the rest of the economy. It matters not whether resources are wasted by propping up 'sunset' industries or by subsidising faddish new technologies which fail to take off. Economic waste is economic waste, however it occurs.

The appropriate role for government in its relations with industry is to avoid as far as possible selective interventions which hamper and distort the process of economic evolution. Its positive role lies in seeking to enhance the general environment so that entrepreneurship and innovation can flourish on their own. The measures proposed here would advance us towards that end.

[74]

TOPICS FOR DISCUSSION

1. 'It is precisely because we do not have perfect information that a market economy, which saves on the information costs of organising a complex economic system, is vital for the task of economic co-ordination.' Discuss.

2. What beneficial role does bankruptcy fulfil?

3. Trace the different routes by which government might finance industrial subsidies and the different taxpayers, consumers, savers and employees who might be made to bear the cost.

4. What forms of subsidy, and under what circumstances, can welfare economics be invoked to justify?

5. Expound and examine critically the 'infant-industry' argument for government assistance.

6. What are the reasons for expecting that government bail-outs of uncompetitive firms may retard their capacity for rejuvenation?

7. Describe and evaluate the principal propositions of the economic theory of politics/public choice.

8. Do you find the concept of the 'political market' useful?

9. Evaluate the author's proposal to give away the ownership rights in loss-making state-owned enterprises to the general public with unlimited liability for the first few years.

10. What, in your view, are the pros and cons of a constitutional rule requiring balanced budgets?

FURTHER READING

The history of British industrial policy over the post-war period is discussed in

Young, S. and Lowe, A. V., *Intervention in the Mixed Economy: The Evaluation of British Industrial Policy 1964-72*, Croom Helm, London, 1974.

Grant, W., *The Political Economy of Industrial Policy*, Butterworth and Co., London, 1982.

Skuse, A., *Government Intervention and Industrial Policy*, Heinemann Educational Books, London, 1972.

However, these texts are descriptive and lack economic analysis. Despite the major importance of government policy towards industry, economic analyses of industrial policy are comparatively rare. Those most relevant for this *Hobart Paper* are:

Curzon-Price, V., *Industrial Policy in the European Community*, Macmillan, London, 1981.

Wiseman, J., 'Is There a Logic of Industrial Subsidisation?', in K. Häuser (ed.), *Subsidies, Tax Reliefs and Prices*, Editions Cujas, Paris, 1981.

Rowley, C. K., 'Industrial Policy in the Mixed Economy', in E. Roll (ed.), *The Mixed Economy*, Macmillan, London, 1982, pp. 35-57.

International aspects of industrial policy are discussed in:

Hindley, B., 'The Mixed Economy in an International Context', in E. Roll (ed.), *op. cit.*, pp. 187-205.

Denton, G., O'Cleireacain, S., and Ash, S., *Trade Effects of Public Subsidies to Private Enterprise*, Macmillan, London, 1975.

Other IEA publications of relevance are:

Jewkes, J., *Government and High Technology,* Occasional Paper 37, 1972.

McEnery, J. H., *Manufacturing Two Nations,* Research Monograph 36, 1981.

Papps, Ivy, *Government and Enterprise,* Hobart Paper 61, 1975.

The notion of economic evolution, central to this *Paper,* is explored in:

Alchian, A. A., 'Uncertainty, Evolution, and Economic Theory', *Journal of Political Economy,* Vol. 58, 1950, pp. 211-21.

Nelson, R. R., and Winter, S. G., *An Evolutionary Theory of Economic Change,* Harvard University Press, Cambridge, Mass., 1982.

SOME IEA PUBLICATIONS ON INDUSTRIAL POLICY AND THE ECONOMICS OF POLITICS

Hobart Paper 98
The Birth of Enterprise
An analytical and empirical study of the growth of small firms
MARTIN BINKS and JOHN COYNE
1983   £2·00

Hobart Paperback 9
The Vote Motive
GORDON TULLOCK
with a Commentary by Morris Perlman
1976   2nd Impression 1978   £1·50

Readings 23
Prime Mover of Progress
The entrepreneur in capitalism and socialism
SIR FRANK McFADZEAN, LESLIE HANNAH, P. D. HENDERSON,
ISRAEL KIRZNER, SIR ARTHUR KNIGHT, D. G. MacRAE,
NEIL McKENDRICK, IVOR PEARCE, ARTHUR SELDON,
NIGEL VINSON
1980   £3·50

Readings 18
The Economics of Politics
JAMES M. BUCHANAN, CHARLES K. ROWLEY, ALBERT
BRETON, JACK WISEMAN, BRUNO FREY, A. T. PEACOCK,
and seven other contributors. Introduced by JO GRIMOND
1978   £3·00

Research Monograph 36
Manufacturing Two Nations
*The sociological trap created by the bias of British regional
policy against service industry*
J. H. McENERY
1981   £1·50

Hobart Paper 78
The Consequences of Mr Keynes
JAMES M. BUCHANAN, JOHN BURTON and R. E. WAGNER
1978   £1·50

IEA OCCASIONAL PAPERS in print

*Wincott Memorial Lectures